# Fabulous Fabrications from Busted Hockey Gear

Also by Peter Manchester

**50 Things to Make with a Broken Hockey Stick**

# Fabulous
# Fabrications
## from Busted Hockey Gear

## PETER MANCHESTER

Edited by Rhona Sawlor.
Cover illustrations by Peter Manchester.
Cover design by Paul Vienneau.
Book design by Julie Scriver.
Printed in Canada by Transcontinental Printing.
10  9  8  7  6  5  4  3  2  1

Library and Archives Canada Cataloguing in Publication

Manchester, Peter, 1952-
    Fabulous fabrications from busted hockey gear / Peter Manchester.

ISBN 0-86492-413-5

    1. Hockey — Equipment and supplies — Humor.  2. Canadian wit and humor (English)  I. Title.

PN6231.H54M34 2004        C818'.602        C2004-904455-9

Published with the financial support of the Canada Council for the Arts, the Government of Canada through the Book Publishing Industry Development Program, and the New Brunswick Culture and Sports Secretariat.

Goose Lane Editions
469 King Street
Fredericton, New Brunswick
CANADA  E3B 1E5
www.gooselane.com

*To Sheelagh, Elijah,
Sebastien, and Dante*

# Table of Contents

# Rink-incarnation

There is no act more noble than to take something old and used up and give it new life. I'm not talking about just old newspapers, beer bottles and aluminum cans. I believe that almost anything that has been manufactured can find another useful purpose, should we keep the old thinking cap on long enough. Even items that have been previously recycled may still have more life in them. I am just as guilty as anyone of putting out more garbage than I feel one family could possibly generate in a week. I feel bad as I slink back from the curb, waiting for the town to cart it all away to the landfill. It amazes me that we design in only singular uses for our artifacts and gizmos. We have been preached to about the benefits of multi–tasking, so why not apply that way of thinking to the way we use things every day? I am putting forward the idea of "pre-cycling" — finding multiple uses for our wares before and after their intended use.

Before my first book, *50 Things to Make with a Broken Hockey Stick*, came out, I used to be able to go down to the rink and get armloads of used-up sticks all the time. Now other people stop by several times a week to collect them. On my last trip, all I found was a pitiful single stick. Are people staking up their tomatoes in February in New Brunswick? The other possibility is that hockey stick recycling has really caught on. I asked, why stop at hockey sticks? Why not look at all hockey equipment as fodder? Needing to expand my horizons due to limited stick resources, for the past year or so, I have been researching the exciting field of putting all kinds of busted hockey equipment to work. Oh, if only I could find a broken Zamboni . . .

Ice-rink-bound denizens are fortunate. First of all, there is a heck of a lot of broken stuff lying about, and I don't mean just water fountains. Sticks, gloves, helmets and padding all break, lose parts or just start smelling so bad that they are given to a younger sibling to deal with. Or worse, they're put in an old equipment bag and left to fester until the next yard sale. Luckily, hockey equipment has lots and lots of parts — great parts with wacky shapes, materials and functionality. Parts that you can experiment and create with.

I am proposing a process called "rink-incarnation." A wonderland of construct-o-rama experiences awaits the devoted rink junk collector. There is the possibility of furnishing your house, making *objets d'art*, developing complex mechanical models, and discovering the physics of sticks. Many of the old mechanical chestnuts such as levers, fulcrums, and pivot points will be revisited in this book. Lucky for your household, there is nothing here that makes explosions or farting noises on command. Those already exist in most homes under the label of "brother" or, in my case, me.

Rest assured that no Natural Sciences and Engineering Research Council grants were given in the area of my study. In fact, this convenient manual was produced solely out of a simple love of fooling around with items at hand. There is always room for more inquisitive minds in this world. As anyone who has spent time experimenting knows, experiments often result in big piles of cut-up stuff that don't do anything. The spirit of experimentation is cumulative. Knowledge and experience build incrementally until you are a stud-muffin creating machine. At this point in life, I only wish that were true. I do know that if your brain keeps working on a problem, you will be amazed at all the different solutions that come pouring forth. Even though most of our possessions seem to be electronic battery-burning doodads, we can still cherish the earlier mechanical sounds of things that whir and pop.

I was recently asked to see if I could get an old grandfather clock to work. It was an amazing thing to behold. All the gears looked as if they had been individually machined. The housing was a box of hand cut wood, imperfect in dimension but endearing in personality. The cuckoo mechanism was a clever set of weighted bellows and springs. After a few adjustments, all it took to keep the clock going was the daily lifting of its weights, as the clock was made without coil springs. The regulating mechanism of an old clock is the result of hundreds of years of knowledge, with the occasional small addition of a different and sometimes better way of doing things. Nothing is static in an old clock. There is stored energy and released energy, the play of gravity and centrifugal force. An old clock like this is truly a wonder of applied mechanics — amazingly accurate, no battery required. I would have been happy to have seen this type of thing included in a deep space probe as a testimonial to our civilization, rather than a space-age compilation of circuit boards and chips. It is in this spirit that I present this book. I want to encourage folks to get cracking with experimentation and start building stuff. I want readers to take what I have come up with and make it better. Plug in your own ideas and make improvements. Just do it safely. Put away the electronics and the video games. Get out the tools and get thee to a workbench. This is when we come alive, when we create.

## A Note About Angles

ON A CHOP SAW, THE 90° ANGLE CUT IS INDICATED AS 0°. I HAVE INDICATED ALL CUTS AS THEY WOULD BE ON A PROTRACTOR. FOR EXAMPLE, A 70° CUT WOULD BE 20° ON A CHOP SAW.

# Crouching Dog, Hidden Menace

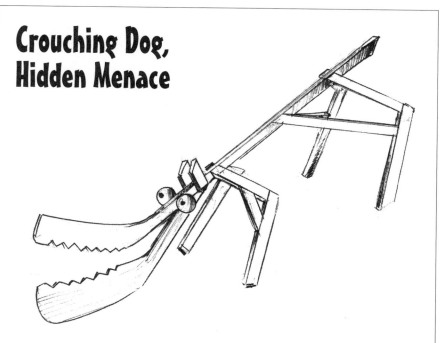

**N**ow you can finally have a nice quiet pet that never requires feeding or walking or poop-scooping. All you need is two hockey sticks with blades, three without, a 1 1/2" piece of 1/4" dowel, wood glue (or quick-setting epoxy), wood screws (1 1/2" and 2"), and two round wooden drawer pulls for eyeballs. Tools required are a drill for making pilot holes, some clamps and a saw. A scroll saw might come in handy here, but only if you are using all-wood sticks (reinforced sticks will dull your saw blades). Use a vise for some of these cuts, because you will be working with some odd angles. You will also need a protractor to measure these angles, all given as smaller than 90°, for the sake of simplicity. Check the diagrams for orientation.

To make this guy look frisky and ready for play, he needs to be crouching. This means you'll have to make a lot of very weird cuts. The body stick is the easiest, so let's start there. 30" above from the curve of the blade, cut the stick handle at a 20° angle towards the bottom of the stick to form a pointed tail. From here on, things are going to get a little trickier, so keep the diagram handy.

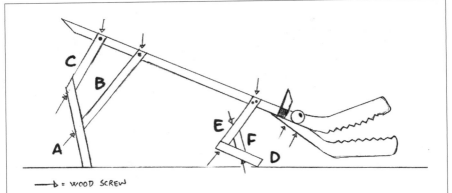

—▶ = WOOD SCREW

Now let's do one leg at a time, starting at the back. There are three pieces to each leg, one 10 1/2" long (A), one 11 1/2" long (B), and one 7" long (C). The A piece is cut at 65° where it meets the floor and 23° at the knee. The B piece has a 20° cut where it meets A and 40° where it meets the body. The leg flares out from the body, and this requires a tapered cut of 20° 1/4" from the edge of the stick (see diagram). The C piece has a cut of 77° where it meets the lower leg and another compound cut at the other end: cut it at 43° to match the line of the back and then at 12° 1/4" from the edge of the stick. Attach B and C to A as illustrated with 2" wood screws and wood glue. Now make the other back leg. When it is completed and assembled, clamp both legs in place and check for position and fit. Don't attach them yet though — make the front legs next.

¼" WIDE

Front leg pieces are D, 8" long; E, 6 3/4" long; and F, 2" long. Cut D with a 90° chop on both ends. Cut E at 70° on one end and 65° where it will attach to the body. The front legs also flare out, and this requires a second cut on E where it meets the body. Make this cut at 22° 1/4" from the edge (see diagram). The elbow needs additional support, with F cut at 55° on each side. Assemble with wood screws and glue.

The lower jaw is a blade that has the teeth forms cut out, and it is mounted to the lower edge of the body. Experiment with how open you want the jaw to be. I found 10° to my liking. Cut the teeth on the upper jaw so that they correspond with the lower teeth. Attach the lower jaw to the body with two 1 1/2" wood screws and wood glue.

Now clamp the legs in position to check for fit and appearance. The lower jaw should be about 1" off the floor. When all looks good, drill some pilot holes, and then add glue to joining faces, and use 1" screws to attach the legs to the body. The front legs will require two short screws per side. You need to place these strategically; the trick is to avoid hitting the screws coming from the other side.

The ears are two pieces cut 3" long. The ear tops are cut at 65°, so that the slope is seen from the front. The lower portion of the ear is cut at 45° on the narrow side of the stick. Glue these into position, using clamps to hold them till the glue dries. Epoxy is the best choice here. The eyes are drilled with a 1/4" bit halfway in towards the centre of the ball. Find a good eye position above the upper jaw and drill a hole there also. Paint the eyeballs white, and glue in position with wood glue and 1/4" dowel.

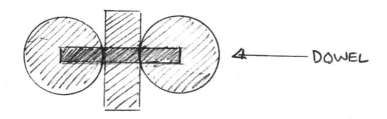

After the eyes are in place, cut two 1/2" circles of black paper and use these to determine the best placement for the pupils. Once you've decided, draw them on with a permanent marker.

All those cuts are a pain, but believe me, the end product will be worth it — although, come to think of it, the no-nonsense spouse of this household has moved my nice new dog from the front hall to the basement . . .

# Standing Dog, No Dander

have made several of these critters and find that they are a good exercise in woodcraft. A few weird cuts are required, but nothing like the ones needed to make the Crouching Dog. You will need four 36" long hockey stick shafts, all in good shape, and one stick in excellent shape with a 30" long shaft and the blade still attached. The tools you will need are a saw, a drill with a 1/2" bit and a 1/8" bit, some clamps, and some quick-setting epoxy.

It is best to start with the body stick, A. Cut this piece at a 20° angle, 30" from the blade to form a pointed tail. To attach the eyes, drill a 1/2" hole through the blade in the appropriate eye position. Use a 1/2" wooden ball from the hardware store and insert it in a 1/2" hole drilled through the blade so that one half of the ball protrudes on each side of the face. Paint it white before installing, but wait until it is in place to paint on the pupil. Drill another hole with the same 1/2" bit further down toward the tip of the blade to form a nostril. The ears are two pieces cut 3 1/2" long at 45° at both sides. Don't put these on until the legs and lower supports are fully installed.

The legs (B) are 18" long and cut square across the bottom and at 80° (along the narrow edge) where they join the body. If you are up to the challenge of some delicate surgery, cut down only as far as the body stick is deep, and then cut in horizontally to form a lap joint that will give more support when the two pieces are joined. The two crosspieces (C) for the sides are 16" long and cut to 80°, the front crosspiece (D) is about 4" long, and the back one (E) is about 3" long. Wait to cut D and E to get exact measurements and angles once the legs have been installed.

Put the two sets of legs together with the 16" supports (C), using 2"

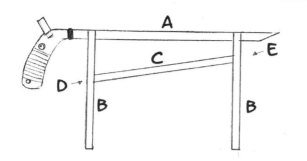

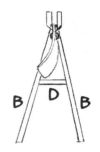

wood screws. Take this assembly and mount it to the body stick. Use clamps while setting this up, drill pilot holes, and put some wood glue in the joint before assembly. The pilot holes should be off-centre, as you don't want the screws hitting each other from either side. Take care to keep the front and back legs parallel to each other, an equal distance apart at top and bottom. When all four legs are attached, gingerly set the structure on the ground to see that all four legs are in contact. At the point where the lower supports (C) meet the front legs, mark off the exact distance and angle on a piece of stick and cut it so that it will go across horizontally directly between the C pieces. Do this again for the back, noting that the back will be shorter as it is higher. Attach these using glue and wood screws, being careful not to hit the other screws holding the outside supports. Let the glue dry and cure before attaching the ears.

The ears can be put on with wood glue, epoxy or a piece of wooden dowel drilled through and glued. For my final flourish, I hot glued

some screw hardware from a helmet to a piece of old chin strap and made a fearsome spiked collar. Be creative.

You could make a whole series of these dogs and line the front hall with them, like the lions that guarded the gates of Babylon. If you're not that ambitious, how about standing two of them side by side and placing something flat across their backs — laminated hockey sticks, for example — to make a dandy coffee table.

# Semi-Salmon

**P**utting a broken goalie stick to use can be a challenge. Besides using one to stir a large vat of gruel or as a quick substitute for a canoe paddle, I was at a loss for ideas. Then I started looking at creatures I could assemble and came up with this fish.

A quick note about goalie sticks. Many are made with long ribbons of carbon fibre or fibreglass to reinforce the wood. These add a great deal of strength to a stick, but alas, they are very hard on the blade that cuts them. I would suggest that you look for a goalie stick that has a wood core with little else added. This is the kind of stick most likely to be found broken and abandoned at the rink, anyway. Besides the goalie stick, you'll also need the blade from a regular stick to put the finishing touches on this fish. A coping saw may be substituted for a scroll saw.

Cut off the blade before the curve so that it yields a straight segment. At the other end, cut it just beyond where the handle flares out to a broad paddle. The body itself is about 19" long. Cut out a tail shape on a scroll saw, and then taper the forward end, leaving a 2 1/4" edge on which to epoxy the head. Draw the fins out on the excess part of the blade, then cut them out with a scroll saw. The salmon has a heck of a lot of fins. There are the two dorsal fins (first and second), two gill fins, two pectoral fins, two pelvic fins, two anal fins and a caudal fin. I decided to make my fish two dimensional, meaning I only had to cut one of each kind of fin. I also shaved down the piece for the gill fin so that it would be thinner and lie closer to the body. Sand the fin pieces before attaching them. Glue to the body with quick-setting epoxy.

The head is comprised of two pieces of stick handle, each cut to 7". Cut a mouth opening along a 5" arc. The teeth are cut from the blade of a regular hockey stick. Mark out a series of similar triangles along the edge of the blade and cut them out. These are also epoxied on along the curve of the mouth opening. Leaving on some of the residual tape matter will give the fish a more rogue-like appearance.

For the eye, use a 3/4" wooden ball attached with a dowel and wood glue.

For the ambitious modeller, may I suggest making this fish in full 3D detail, with fins on both sides, then mounted on a metal rod and base. There you have it, a trophy fish that you made by yourself, without causing harm to a single sentient being, assuming you were careful with your saw. This is one salmon you do not have to release when caught, but it is quite lacking in nutritional value.

# Trophy Spikefish

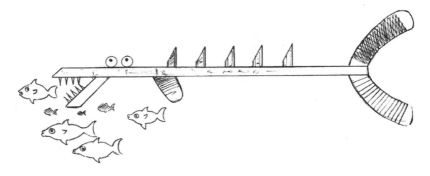

**H**aving this anatomically ambivalent beast on display will liven up any wall. It is similar to those finned denizens of darkness that live and feed in deep ocean canyons.

To make this fish you will need two hockey stick shafts, one at least 38" long with a blade still attached, two more blades, a length of dowel, two wooden balls, some quick-setting epoxy, wood glue, some 2" wood screws, two eyehooks and some picture-hanging wire. The only tools you'll need are a coping saw or hand saw and a drill.

Begin with cutting the dorsal spikes. You will need five or six of them, cut on a 20° angle. This can be a tough job using a chop saw for this due to the fact that those convenient angles end at 45°. So, put the stick in a vise and make the cuts with a handsaw. Use all-wood sticks so your saw blade will remain sharp.

You need to cut the blades that will form the tail fins so that they match in size and angle. Line the blades up against each other, and when they look even, mark out a cut line on the blades and saw it as straight as possible. For the pelvic fin, you need only about 5" of blade, but try to cut it on the same angle as the tail fins. The jaw is a piece 5 1/2" long, cut on a 45° angle. The body has a 45° cut at its end to give your fish a sharp nose. Now make the teeth. Sharpen the end of a length of 1/4" dowel in a pencil sharpener, then cut it off 1/4" behind the taper. Repeat eight more times to make nine teeth in all. Set aside.

Use small wooden balls from the hardware store for eyes. With a 1/8" bit, drill a hole 3/4" deep in each ball. Put two screws through a piece of scrap wood so that the tips protrude. Twist the eyeballs onto these protrusions so they'll stay in place while you paint them. Apply two coats of white paint, allowing drying time between each.

Drill pilot holes for the dorsal spikes every 3" along the underside of the shaft, starting 14" from the nose. Glue and screw in dorsal spikes from below. Place the lower jaw in position along the main shaft so that the mouth looks even. Clamp in place and drill a pilot hole for the screw that will secure it. Before you attach it, however, use a 1/4" drill bit and drill out evenly spaced tooth sockets. Drill five holes on the lower jaw and four on the upper. Set the teeth in place with wood glue.

Eye placement gives a face its character. Play around with the arrangement until you're satisfied, and then drill pilot holes for the eye screws. The placement of the pupil on the eyes will change the expression of the fish. A little experimentation in this matter will also provide great hilarity. The smaller the iris, the meaner the fish will look.

At this point you can attach all the parts that go on with screws. When you're finished, it's time to attach the tail and pelvic fins. These need to be epoxied on. Do a dry run to figure out the best way to hold everything in place while the epoxy cures. Do one side at a time. If you are using clamps, make sure to keep the epoxy off them. You will need to mix a batch about the volume of a marble to cover the base of each fin. Apply to one fin at a time and carefully set in place. These should be left alone as they cure. Repeat until all three are in place. Install the eye hooks and hanging wire behind the fish at the beast's balancing point. And there you have it: a finished famished fish.

# Big-Jawed Buddyfish

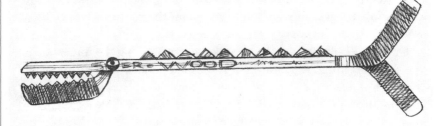

Those busted-up hockey stick blades make some kind of great jaw. Kirk Douglas should have such a jaw. A big chompin' vise of a jaw. A jaw you will think about next time you are out for a long swim in the ocean.

Here is what you will need to make this fish: one hockey stick with the blade still attached; two more blades that are in decent shape or that can be stiffened up with some hockey tape; a hockey stick handle shaft about 12" long or more; a 1 1/2" wooden ball; some quick-setting epoxy. You will also need a coping saw or scroll saw and a drill.

Take the broken hockey stick that you will use for the body. 34" beyond the blade cut the handle at 45°. Cut one of the remaining blades 4" up the shaft. This will be the lower tail fin. Tape both of these blades so that they look similar. Next, take your remaining blade and place it in the jaw position. When it has the angle of chomp that you desire, mark a line across the blade that will indicate where to cut. Make the cut as straight as possible. Before you attach the jaw, cut out the teeth. Teeth are 1/2" high. A quick way to draw these is to mark a line 1/2" away from the top edge of the blade. Do a zigzag indicating the cuts, keeping the teeth similar. Cut these out with a saw and save the cut-out pieces to use as the upper teeth. Of course you can take great liberties with the teeth, so if you have a better idea, go for it.

For the dorsal spine, cut nine pieces of hockey stick at 45°, so that you have nine equilateral triangles.

Paint the wooden ball white to make the eyeball, and make the eyelid out of hockey tape. Draw on the pupil. The size is up to you, but you could start small and then enlarge them to suit your whim.

To assemble all this, lay the main shaft on its narrow side, blade up. Take the dorsal spine pieces and arrange them to your liking. They look best if they are symmetrical. Please read all instructions on the epoxy container for using the product safely. Apply the epoxy, place spines and let set.

Take the lower tail fin and attach it, from the back side of the fish, with two 1" wood screws. Next, place the jaw in the desired position and attach likewise. If you want to have a moveable jaw, use only one screw. Take the triangles that you cut out of the jaw blade and prepare them so that there is a clean surface that will be glued to the shaft. Removal of hockey tape is up to you. The more tape, the funkier the teeth will appear. Place the fish on its back. Mix a batch of epoxy and carefully glue the teeth in place. Let this set.

Eye position is a judgement call. I find that the closer the eye is to the jaw, the more predatory the fish looks. Attach the eye from the back of the fish with a 1 1/4" wood screw. Find the balancing point of this piece, put eye hooks 1" on either side of this point, and put on some picture hanging wire. Find a suitable wall and hang up your lean, mean chomping machine.

# Scorpion

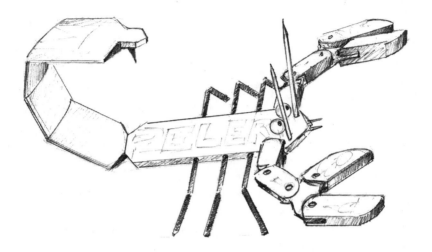

**G**oalie hockey sticks have always been a conundrum when it comes to after-breakage use. Yes, they are wonderfully paddle-like, useful for canoeing or disciplinary purposes. But I believe I have finally got the inside lane in this fiercely competitive world of busted stickdom. A goalie stick really does make an excellent scorpion to add to any wooden menagerie.

You will need two broken goalie sticks, a handle shaft of a regular all-wood hockey stick, a 48" length of 1/4" dowel, and two 3/4" wooden balls for eyes. You'll also need a small piece of 1/4" plywood measuring 1" x 4" for the pincers. Tools required are a scroll saw or jigsaw, a power saw that can do compound cuts, a drill with a 1/4" bit, and a pencil sharpener. Finally, you'll need some quick-setting epoxy.

There are two tricky parts to this project, the tailpiece and the pincers. The tailpiece has fewer parts, so let's start there. Take one of the goalie stick blades. Set the compound saw to 60°. Cut the first length at 60°, 4 1/2" from the handle. Cut the handle at 45°, then form a point with another 45° cut from the other side, 1" up from the blade. Cut two more pieces 3 1/2" long at the same 60° angle, flipping the blade with each cut so that

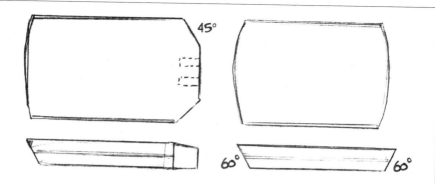

the angles taper towards each other. The last piece is 4 1/2" long, with a 60° cut at one end and an 80° cut at the other, where it connects to the body. This last piece requires a 45° cut on each side of the blade towards the centre, 1" down from the corner edge. This will make it look like a segmented tail connection. Cut another section of goalie stick 10" long. Where the tail meets the body, do the same angled cut as on the last tail piece. At the other end, make two cuts 30° towards the centre. These cuts should come to a point where the head will be.

You must put the tail section together incrementally. Epoxy the tail sections together before attaching the tail to the body. Do this over wax paper or something that won't be ruined if the epoxy drips. You will need to prop up the tail to hold it in position until the epoxy sets. After the first piece sets, work your way around the tail to the end piece. Before you attach the final tail piece, however, drill a hole 1/4" deep on the inside part of the tail at the point where the handle meets the blade. This will hold the "stinger" of the scorpion (which you and I know is just a piece of dowel you sharpened in the pencil sharpener, but it still looks pretty impressive). Attach this last tailpiece with epoxy.

The connecting surface at the tail is cut at 80°, giving this section a slight perky rise. Secure this connection with two pieces of 1/4" dowel, 1 1/2" in length. Drill two holes 3/4" deep in the connecting tail surface and likewise in the body, accommodating for the angle of the tail. These dowel pieces will greatly strengthen this union. Epoxy the dowel and the connecting tail section, and let this piece cure thoroughly.

Now make the pincer parts. These should be approached in three steps: first the section that attaches to the body, then the middle section, and, finally, the pincers. The mechanism of the front arms has four pivot points that swivel on pieces of dowel: two at the pincers and one at each end of the middle section. Piece A is cut on one end to fit on the profile of the body and has a tab cut on the other so that it allows piece B to swivel. B has slots cut in both sides to accommodate the tab in A and the pincer mounting plate, C. B is cut round on one end and arced on the other to stop it from swivelling backwards. The mounting plate, C, is cut from 1/4" plywood and requires three holes (see illustration), slightly larger

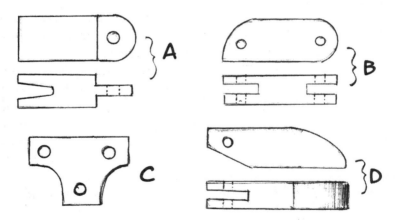

than the dowel so it can rotate freely. Just keep the drill running and bore the holes out smooth, and that should make them large enough. The pincers (D) are mirror images of each other (one left, one right). For each arm, cut four pieces of dowel to 3/4". Assemble prior to gluing to check for fit and movement. The dowel should be glued only at the outer points, and the epoxy should be kept off the pivot tab of A and piece C (see illustration). Mount the arms to the body when the epoxy is set.

Drill holes in the wooden balls (eyes) so that they can be mounted with a 3/4" length of dowel to the body. Just in front of the eyes and angled outwards, drill two more holes for the antennae. Drill two more holes in the front of the head for the mouth parts. Using the pencil sharpener, sharpen one end of the dowel, cut off a piece the right length for a mouth part or antenna, then sharpen the end again. Then cut off another piece, and so on, until you have enough mouth parts and antennae. Antennae are 5 1/4" long, and you'll need 2 of them. Mouth parts are 1" long, and you'll need 2. Glue them into the appropriate holes. Find the balancing point of the whole structure. Drill the centre leg holes at that point, and drill the others 1 1/4" apart on each side of the centre hole. Drill these six holes (three per side) with a 1/4" bit as straight as possible into the edge of the body. This procedure can be tricky, so use a vise, and drill pilot holes first.

The legs are made from six 2 3/4" pieces of dowel protruding from the bottom of the body, each of which has a 3" piece of dowel attached at the end, forming a "knee joint" that is angled between 60° and 90° to simulate a walking posture. Use sandpaper on the ends of the dowels to vary the angle of each connection. Epoxy the leg pieces together on a flat surface and let them cure thoroughly. Before epoxying the finished legs in place, insert them in the holes in the body and sand carefully to even out the leg ends so that the scorpion won't wobble when completed. Insert the legs into the body and swivel them back and forth to test the effect. When you are satisfied, epoxy them in place. Now, all that is left to do is paint the legs black and the eyes white. Experiment with the placement of pupils using a black paper dot. When you have found the best expression, paint the pupil on with black paint or a permanent marker.

If your scorpion is back heavy, insert a small piece of dowel vertically into the body near the back end to hold the beast up.

Needless to say, this bug will not stand up to extreme play. It is an *objet d'art*. Treat it as such, and it will withstand years of admiration.

# Snakes

I have always thought that hockey stick companies should use snakes in their advertising. Snakes are cunning and quick, and they sneak about, striking with accuracy. Aren't those the attributes of a good forward? Why don't we see cobras and mambas on the graphics of hockey stick companies? Well, you might say that snakes shun the cold and like to find warm spots in the sun. The same might be said of some Canadians.

I love making snakes from hockey sticks. It is pretty simple, just requiring a lot of cutting, unless of course you make a very straight, rigid snake. In that case, just add the eyes to the stick, and bada-bing, you're done. But, assuming you are up to the challenge, I'm offering two designs that call for some cutting and assembling.

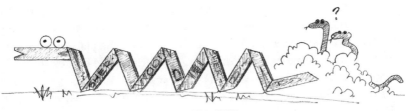

CRUISING SNAKE

# Display Snake

start by cutting a hockey stick into 5" segments, with 60° cuts on one end and 45° cuts on the other. Arrange these in interesting patterns. Then cut a piece of stick a little shorter than the body pieces for the tail, and cut one more piece, this time with a square cut at one end, for the head.

60°  45°

Arrange this model so that like angles connect to your liking. Connect the joints by pre-drilling, inserting some wood glue, then screwing them together. I used one 1 1/4" drywall screw per joint, and this snake is still is holding up well, even in a household of three energetic boys!

You can make your snake look like a cobra by simulating that fan gizmo they flare out when they are alarmed. Simply cut two pieces at 45° angles on each end and attach them to the sides of the head. Use 1" wooden balls for eyes, mounted on pieces of dowel. Of course, snakes do not have eyes on the backs of their heads, like this design does. Did Picasso's models have both eyes on the same side of their noses? Feel free to cast aside reality in the pursuit of fine craft.

# Cruising Snake

This snake is a cruising-around-minding-his-own-business type of creature. Cut ten pieces 5" long, with a 45° cut at each end. This uses up the shaft of one broken stick. For the head, cut a piece square on one end and at 60° on the other. For the mouth, make a V cut at the square end with a scroll saw. For the tail, attach two pieces matching the 45° cuts. Then attach all the other pieces together as illustrated. I pre-drilled the holes and used 1 1/4" sheetrock screws with a bit of wood glue for good measure, and I tried to put the screws in spots where they would not be readily seen by the admiring public. It is way easier to sand the edges, if you are so inclined, before assembly.

Of course, you may choose to alternate pieces cut from different sticks and thus create an amazing colour scheme. You can make the snake as long as you wish, but remember that the longer the snake, the greater the stress on the joints. Feel free to experiment with different arrangements of pieces, too.

For eyes, use 1" wooden balls from the hardware store. Paint them white and draw the pupils with a marker or paint. The shape and style of the pupils is what gives this beast its character, and you can get great entertainment value from your experiments. Do them with paper dots first: covering marker requires multiple coats of paint. Attach the eyes to the body using lengths of dowel set with glue. You might consider varnishing the installed eyeballs to add lustre.

To mount your snake on the wall, use two eye hooks and a length of picture wire. A single snake on the wall gets pretty lonely, though, so you should make lots of them.

# Shore Bird on a Stand

This bird is easy to make, and I think it's quite adorable. You will need 12" of all-wood stick and two 1 3/4" long pieces of 3/16" dowel. You will also need wood glue or quick-setting epoxy. Tools required are a drill with a 3/16" bit and a saw.

Cut a piece of stick 3" long, then cut it corner to corner along the wide side of the stick. This will give you two triangular wing pieces with an angle of about 20° at the tips. Now cut a piece of stick 3 1/2" long for the body. Using a wing piece as a template, cut this 3 1/2" piece lengthwise at the same angle. This will leave a 1/2" straight section at the end, which is where the wings will be attached. Take the piece you've just cut off and cut the end at 45° to make the head. Then cut that off at 90°, 1 1/4" from the end. For the beak, cut another piece at a 45° angle, and from that protruding angle cut the end 3/4" up and at an angle of 10° (see illustration). Sand off the ends of the wings so that they are rounded, then sand a crescent indentation at the tip of the tail.

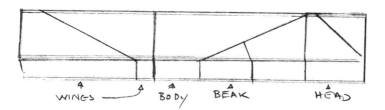

WINGS     BODY     BEAK     HEAD

For the base, cut a piece of stick 4 1/2" long. Now this part is kind of tricky. The holes you are about to drill will be at an angle to give your creation a bird-like stance. Drill two holes 1 1/2" back from the front of the base and 1/2" apart. They should be angled about 20° off vertical towards the back of the stand. The underbody should be drilled at the same angle 1 1/4" back from the front of the body. The lower body and the stand should be parallel when assembled.

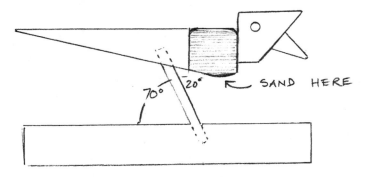

To assemble, start by gluing or epoxying the wings to the body. This is easily done by turning the body and wings upside down and gluing them together on a flat surface. Let the glue dry. With sandpaper, round out the spot where the lower portion of the wings meet the body so that it is smooth and flush. When all is set up, put a clothespin on the tail to hold the bird face-up. Glue the head on so that it is set back from the bottom edge of the bird by 1/4". When that is set up, find a book or something about 2" high and lean the bird back, so that the lower surface of the head is horizontal. Glue the bottom of the beak in the middle of this area. After that is dry, put a dab of wood glue in each hole where the dowel will go for the legs, assemble, then let dry. Paint a tiny eye on each side of the head. Now you have a cute little bird ready for domicile adornment or gift-gifting.

# Rocking Bird

**M**ake the Shore Bird, but instead of putting it on a base, make a rocking platform to mount the bird on. Cut two 6" long rockers out of wooden hockey sticks. Using wood screws, attach a 3" cross piece between the rockers. Drill a 1/4" hole at the centre of the cross piece to insert a piece of 1/4" dowel. Drill a matching hole in the base of the bird for the other end of the dowel. Mount the bird on the dowel, sand the rockers smooth and you're done.

WINGS — BODY  BEAK    HEAD    ROCKER

# Pelican

This noble bird will grace any wall and look way cooler than those plaster Canada geese that one sees in rec rooms across the nation. This guy's goofy, he's big, and he has attitude.

To fabricate this pelican, you will need four hockey sticks with blades still somewhat intact. Make sure one of the sticks has 28" of handle, and that the other three have 10" each. You will also need two more blades that are relatively intact, wood glue, some quick-setting epoxy, an inch of 1/4" dowel, four wood screws, and two 1 1/2" wooden balls. Tools needed include a saw and drill. Keep an eye out for old feathers to use for decoration. I always seem to come across stray crow feathers for some reason, so I used them.

Take the longer stick and cut it 28" up the handle at a 45° angle. Then cut the end of the stick blade with a deep V-notch to simulate tail feathers (see illustration). Take three of the remaining sticks and arrange them so that the blades nestle beneath each other. These three blades will simulate the wings. The blades are tilted 65° relative to the shaft. Set these so that the upper wing shaft projects 10" beyond the body. Place the other two blades below this one so that the handle shafts are parallel. Draw a guideline across these three shafts where they meet the body, then make your cut along that line.

Drill pilot holes in the appropriate spots from beneath, and attach the three wing pieces from the bottom with wood screws. Drill a series of holes in the shortest wing piece to hold the quills of the miscellaneous feathers that you have collected. Affix these with wood glue.

The lower jaw of the pelican is cut from a stick blade. Place the piece so that the upper part of the blade is parallel to the shaft (see illustration), leaving 1/2" space between them. Draw a line to so you can make the cut as straight as possible. Outline with a pencil and then cut the bottom edge of the blade to resemble the shape of a pelican's bill. Attach the lower jaw piece with wood glue and a wood screw from the top. Cut out a dozen 1/2" high triangles from the remaining blade to make the teeth. An avian purist will tell you that pelicans have no teeth. Of course they are correct, so acknowledge their intelligence and show them the door. This isn't that kind of pelican. Apply the epoxy to the cut edge of the triangles to get the best bond, and affix the teeth. You can leave them as is, wrapped with the old hockey tape, or paint them the colour of your choice. I gave mine yellow teeth.

With a 1/4" bit, drill holes 1/2" deep in the two 1 1/2" wooden balls. Then drill two identical holes in a piece of scrap wood. Set the dowels into the balls, and mount them temporarily onto the scrap wood. This will make painting the balls very easy. Use two coats of white paint, letting the eyeballs dry fully between coats. Go back to the pelican's body and drill two 1/2" deep holes 1 1/2" apart just above where the jaw meets the body. When the painted eyeballs are dry, glue them on to the dowel pieces, and then put glue in the holes that you just drilled on the shaft and insert the dowel. There should be no dowel showing. Paint the pupils on so that the eyes look in any direction you want.

To hang the bird, find the balancing point (on the bird I made, it was about half way up the first wing shaft), screw eye hooks on either side, and loop with picture wire.

# Squawking Bird

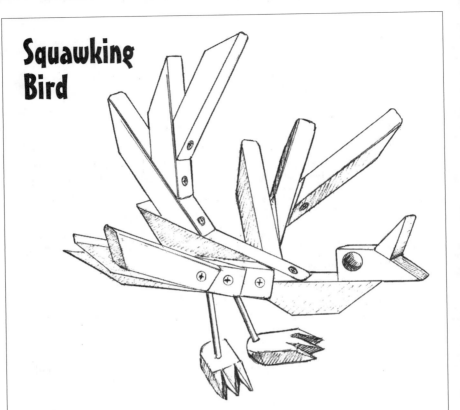

I had a lot of fun creating this bird. I wanted to see if I could simulate feathers with hockey sticks. Of course, you will have to use your own judgement, but I think I succeeded. This project requires one length of hockey stick handle and 6" of 1/4" dowel, a dozen 1" wood screws, two cats-eye marbles and some epoxy. Tools required are a drill for pilot holes, a protractor, a rubber band and a saw. Choose an all-wood hockey stick to reduce wear and tear on your saw blade. You will need a solid work surface to do the drilling on.

There are a lot of cuts here, few of them square. All pieces are mounted on the body, so cut that first. It is 4" long, with a 45° cut on each end. The tail section begins with a 30° cut at one end and a 45° cut at the other end of a 5" piece of stick. The remaining three pieces are 4" long and all have 45° cuts on both ends.

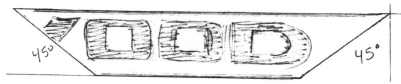

## LAST 3 TAIL PIECES (1ST PIECE 30° AND 45°)

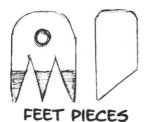

**FEET PIECES**

The feet are cut to simulate talons (see illustration). These will be drilled to hold the dowel, but don't do it just yet, as the angle is yet to be determined. The head is pretty straightforward, with a square cut on one end and a 45° cut on the other. The beak is cut from a 1 1/4" piece with a 20° cut at one end and a square cut on the other.

The wings are cut from 4 1/2" pieces. There are 20° cuts on the narrow side of the stick and a 45° cut on the wide side. Each wing requires three pieces.

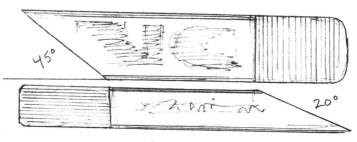

**WING PIECES**

To assemble the bird, build the tail section as illustrated. Drill pilot holes and countersink the screw heads. For the truly adventurous, these connections can be made with wooden dowels and wood glue. The tail should be flat when completed, but not the wings. The wing pieces are put together so that they have an upward sweep. Mount these along the cuts you made to the wide side of the stick. The narrow edge becomes the top of the wing. Rotate each piece 15° relative to the piece it is being attached to. (You can change these angles as you like.)

Drill the head with 3/8" drill bit on either side as "sockets" for the eyes (marbles). Epoxy the head to the front of the body. When this is assembled, epoxy the beak into place. Now you can epoxy the marble eyes into the sockets you've drilled, then hold them in place with a rubber band until set.

Now comes the hard part — figuring out where the bird's balancing point is. The easy way would be to insert the legs vertically, at a 90° angle from the feet. But that is not how real birds' legs attach to the body; they angle up backwards from the feet towards the back of the bird. For this model, I drilled holes at 70° angles in the feet and body, and inserted the dowels. The trick here is to make sure that most of the weight is forward of the feet and the counterbalance is at a point on the first tail piece. This will take a little trial and error to get the right spot for the holes. If you find you have drilled in the wrong place, fill in the holes with dowel pieces and try again. Sand the bottoms of the feet if necessary to make the bird stand up straight.

# Bird on a Rod

"Garden Statuary" evokes semi-clad Greek babes, pouring water from an urn and adorning a formal garden. But imagine instead a construction made of hockey sticks, swaying in the breeze on your own turf. You might make a single bird, or you could make a whole flock. Your garden statuary might even have crow scaring properties.

Here is what you will need for each bird: two blades, one left and one right handed, with at least 5" of shaft. You will also need an additional 24" of all-wood hockey stick shaft; 8" of 1/4" wooden dowel; wood glue; quick-setting epoxy; various wood screws; hockey tape; a piece of steel rod 1/4" in diameter and long enough to make your statue the height you want; and a large rock, preferably sandstone for easier drilling. Tools required are a drill with a 1/4" bit and a 1/4" masonry bit, a mitre saw, a scroll saw, and clamps.

The tough part of this project will be the wings. You need to cut them so that they swoop a little forward and upward. Blades have different lies and curves, so your mission is to find a left and right blade with similar attributes. Cut the shaft 3" beyond the point where the blade ends. Looking towards the front of the bird, the left wing will have a cut of 80° and the right wing 100°. Then make another cut so that the blade also tapers up 15°. The left blade will have a cut of 105° and the right 75° if the blades are jutting upwards. (If you can do one cut to both of these specifications, buddy, you are a pro!) Now that the wings are cut, give them a taping job to make them look alike.

Since you've got your saw out, you might as well cut all the parts for this bird. Assembly instructions will follow. Cut two identical pieces of stick 10" long and at a 45° angle at each end. These will be glued together to form the body. Make another piece 2" long, with 45° angle parallel cuts on each end so that they bevel inwards. This will be the neck. The head is two pieces 2 1/2" long, cut at 90° on one end and 45° on the other. The beak is 2 1/2" long, with a 90° cut on one side and 60° on the other. The feet are two triangles of stick 1" long, cut at 45° on each end. Cut two pieces of dowel 2 3/4" long for the legs. The tail is a 4" piece of shaft, cut in the shape of a feather and then sliced into five equal thin pieces on a scroll saw.

Now, let's put all these pieces together. Mark on the body where the wings will join it. The top of the wing is flush with the bird's back. Attach the wings with screws from the inside of each body piece. The screws will be hidden when the two body pieces are put together. Drill pilot holes through the body piece and into the wing. Mix up a batch of epoxy, enough to cover the end of each wing. Apply the epoxy and then screw the wing in place. Put these bird halves aside where they will set without sagging. When they're ready, mix up enough epoxy to cover one inside surface of the body, apply evenly and clamp the pieces together. Put two 1 1/2" screws through the body to add strength. Let this set.

The head and neck are held in place with pieces of dowel, and

they can be assembled with either wood glue or epoxy. Drill a hole 1/2"
deep at the front of the bird at the centre of the body. Place the neck in position, mark the spot where the dowel will go, and drill a hole in the base
of the neck. Where the head joins the neck, repeat this procedure. The
head can face straight forward or be rotated slightly, as if the bird is looking away. When the head is set and secure, attach the beak in a similar
fashion with dowel and glue. Paint an eye on each side.

Sand the dowel leg pieces at one end so they will taper nicely to the
body. Insert the legs into drilled holes in the feet. Glue this arrangement
together and let it set before gluing it to the body. For the tail, fan out
those feather pieces you cut, then glue them together. When dry, sand the
bottom of the tail so that it is flat. Then glue the tail to the back of the
body.

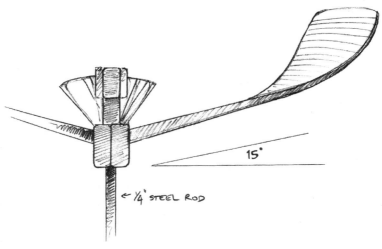

The bird rests on a piece of steel rod inserted into a rock base. Determine how to place the rock so it is stable; it should have a relatively flat
base. Decide where the steel rod will be positioned, and drill a vertical
hole with the masonry bit. Be certain to drill the hole so it's absolutely
vertical. Put the steel rod in the hole, check to make sure it's vertical, and
shim if necessary. Now, using the 1/4" wood bit, drill a hole in the bottom
of the bird at the balancing point. Place the bird on the rod, stand back
and admire while humming that Leonard Cohen song.

# Skate Crow

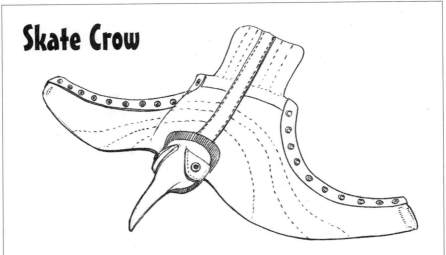

To make this skate-leather crow, you will require one entire skate and a bit of its mate, a sharp X-acto knife and a hot glue gun. To help the bird retain its form, you will also need the oval plastic knee protector from an old shin guard, and some of the felt padding that goes with it. This can be removed by carefully cutting all the stitching with a knife. You will also need the plastic thumb protector found inside an old hockey glove.

You need to remove the leather portion from the base of the skate. Do this very carefully with the X-acto knife. Cut along the point where the leather meets the base of the skate. Don't try to cut it all at once. Make several passes of the blade, scoring deeper with each pass. The segment around the heel is particularly tough, but go easy, take your time, and it will come free. You will need to separate the toe section from the rest. Slice down between the toe piece and the lower eyelet tab through the stitching. The tongue of the skate can be carefully removed from the toe piece by cutting through the stitching. The leather toe piece can be separated from the cardboard toe protector with a bit of effort.

When you have the leather removed from the skate, flatten it out. The upper section that supported the ankle will be the bird's tail. The outstretched side panels become the wings. The tongue of the skate will be formed into the head and beak.

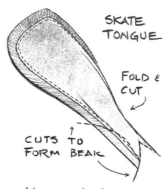

SKATE
TONGUE

FOLD &
CUT

CUTS TO
FORM BEAK

Stretch the skate over the knee protector and check for a satisfactory curve of the bird's back. Mark the position that provides the best shape. With hot glue, go around the circumference of the knee protector and glue this to the inside of the skate in the marked position. The plastic thumb protector from the glove will keep the tail shaped in a nice curve. Cut this thumb protector in two behind the hump, and just use the flat curve. Hot glue this piece in place. If you want a real clean looking lining underside, cut the felt from the shin guards to a shape that will hide the plastic forms, and hot glue it in position.

To make the head, take the tongue of the skate and pinch the edges together 3" from the top (the part not stitched to the toe piece). Determine the beak shape and lightly draw this out on one side with a pencil. Still holding the tongue, cut the beak shape and then hot glue it together. If any hot glue seeps out, let it cool completely and then shave it off with a sharp blade. Hot glue the head in position so that it overlaps the body by at least an inch. Take a piece of felt from the shin guards and roll a shape that will fill out the head cavity beyond the point at which it joins the bird's back. Hot glue this piece in place. If the colour of the head filler contrasts unpleasantly with the other parts of the bird, find a bit of cloth to cover it over and hot glue in position

For eyes, I cut a piece of the eyelet tab from the other skate, with an eyelet forming each eye.

To display the bird, I suggest a piece of dowel inserted vertically in a block of wood. The bird can then be placed on the balancing point and so that it will move subtly with air currents in your home.

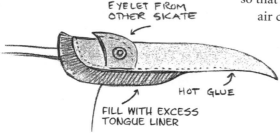

EYELET FROM
OTHER SKATE

HOT GLUE

FILL WITH EXCESS
TONGUE LINER

# Air Punch

'm a nice guy, so I prefer to look at this thing as a celebratory fist-raising device rather than as a sucker-punch demon that can nail a person on the kisser from a good safe distance. To make it, you'll need three stick handles cut into 10 pieces: six 10" pieces, two 11" pieces, and two 16" pieces. You'll also need an old hockey glove, 13 2" bolts with washers, 13 lock nuts, and two cable ties. For tools, you'll need a drill, a 3/16" bit, and a saw.

On the wide side of the 10" stick pieces, drill holes 1" from each end; also drill holes in the centres of the sticks. Drill a hole 1" from one end of each 16" piece. Drill a hole 1" from both ends of each 11" piece.

To assemble, cross the 10" pieces as shown, and drop a bolt through the central hole so they will make a long scissor action. Insert all the bolts in the same direction. Attach the nuts. At one end of this contraption, attach the 16" pieces. Tape the handle ends with hockey tape for a good grip. At the other end, attach one end of each of the 11" pieces, and then bring them together in a point and bolt them. Pull the old hockey glove over the sticks and through the sticks. Fasten the glove on with cable ties. You're done — go out and celebrate.

Do not hit your brother, sister, mom, dad, dog, any unsuspecting stranger, or toads. This implement is intended for rejoicing assistance only.

# Remote Hand Clapper

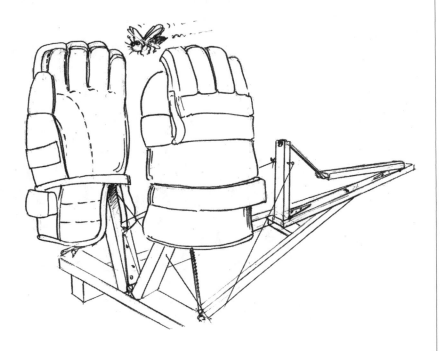

How often have you been overcome with the urge to clap, but your hands were full? This foot-operated clapper will solve that problem. All you need is some hockey sticks, an old pair of hockey gloves, and some basic applied mechanics.

Here is what you will need for this gizmo besides hockey gloves and sticks: three strap hinges 1 1/4" wide and 3 3/4" long; a chin strap from a helmet; two short bungee cords (or springs or rubber bands); two 30" pieces of abrasion-resistant cord; a mix of 1 1/2" and 2" wood screws; and six sturdy eye hooks. You'll also need a drill and a saw. And keep the illustrations handy while you are working so you can refer to them frequently.

The remote hand clapper is built on a triangular base, so make that first. Cut two pieces of stick 18" long (D), and one piece (B) 12" long. Mount B onto the two 18" base pieces from the top. Then cut a piece of stick (F) 16" long, and place it on top of the where the pieces (D) meet at a point, so that it extends 8" beyond. Screw through F into each of the base pieces (D) to hold it for now. Cut a cross piece (G) 2 3/4", long at an 80° angle on either end. Screw G in place from the outside, and then fasten the end of F to G with another screw.

With the base completed, you can now make the clapping mechanism. This is comprised of two stick pieces (A) 12" long. Join the two A pieces along the wide side with one of the strap hinges so that they form a V,

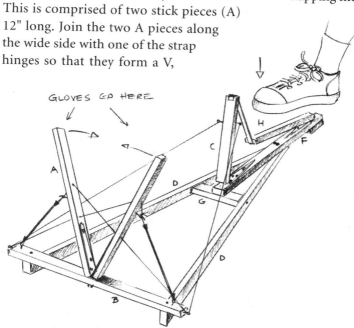

with the hinge at the point. Drill a pilot hole in the centre of the stick pieces at the hinged ends of the A pieces. Next, drill centred holes in each of these pieces 5" and 7" up from the hinged end. At the centre of the cross piece (B), drill or cut out a slot 3/16" wide and 1" long (see illustration). Insert two of the 2" wood screws up from the bottom of the frame. Make sure that they can move freely in this gap, but that the screw heads do not slip through. Screw these in each of the A pieces from the bottom up through the gap. Do not tighten the screws all the way, as these A pieces need to move freely for the hands to clap.

Cut another stick piece (C) 10" long. Attach the second strap hinge to the top of F where the end of the stick joins G. Screw C to the other side of the strap hinge. At the top of C, fasten one end of the chin strap (snaps and chin guard removed) with a screw. Cut a piece of stick 12" long for the pedal (H) and attach it to F with the remaining strap hinge, 1" in from the end of F. The loose end of the chinstrap is screwed in to H from beneath. This is a foot pedal, remember: look for a screw that will not go through to the other side of the stick and into your foot. Put a scrap piece of stick under the end of (F) for support when the pedal is stomped on.

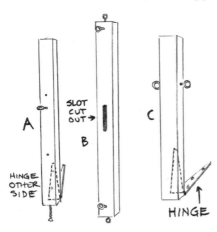

Now comes the fun part, rigging it up. Screw in eye hooks 6" up on the outside of the A pieces, at both ends of the B piece, and 1" in from the ends on the top of B. On piece C put eyehooks on the outside of the stick 6" up. Tie one end of each 30" piece of string to each eye hook on the A pieces, and thread it through the upper hole above the eye hook and across to the lower hole on the opposite A piece. Loop it through the eye hooks on the ends of stick B and over to the eye hooks on piece C. Don't tie it off yet. Hook up the bungees to the eye hooks on pieces A and B. They should not be so taut that it is hard to squeeze the A pieces together. You only need enough tension to pull the pieces apart after H has been depressed. Have the rigging set so that the A pieces are together when H is fully depressed.

Now take out the gloves. The fingers of hockey gloves have a tendency to curl, and they need to be straightened out as much as possible. Try sticking pieces of wood or whatever in them so that they have an open-hand appearance. Once that is done, put them over the A pieces as far as the top hole. Screw them into these pieces, hands facing each other. At this point you should have a hand clapping construction, so fill up your own hands with drinks and snacks and give yourself a raucous round of applause.

# Ice Scooter

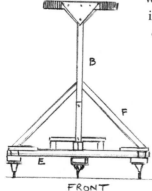

ce scooters have been around since there have been people and blades, or, for that matter, anything with an edge, such as bones, pieces of wood, or frozen fish — no kidding! You can build yourself a basic ice scooter, such as I describe here. Or you could adapt a design that has a steering mechanism with a pivot point at the front connected to a system of pulleys. Another area worth exploring is the use of this scooter as a platform for a traction kite. Speed is assured, and you will attract a crowd of spectators and eager participants. Of course, whatever craft you choose to build, make sure to use it only on ice that you know is safe.

To build this ice scooter, you will need three skates, five or six hockey stick handles with fibreglass reinforcement (strong and stiff), a few scraps of 1/2" plywood, and enough wood screws and nuts and bolts with washers to hold it all together. You will find that in the rigours of propelling yourself, the strains on certain connecting points will stand up best with nuts and bolts. I am referring to the scooter here, not you. Use hockey tape for hand and foot grips.

Build this scooter to the size of the user. Remember, though, that the higher the scooter, the less stable it is, and the greater the stress on the construction. I am not giving measurements, as you can glean relative sizes from the diagrams. The im-

FRONT

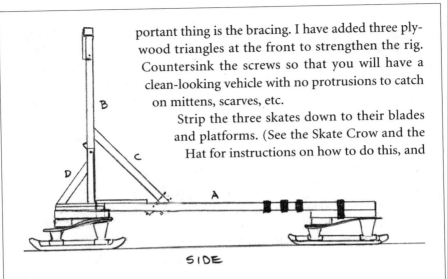

portant thing is the bracing. I have added three plywood triangles at the front to strengthen the rig. Countersink the screws so that you will have a clean-looking vehicle with no protrusions to catch on mittens, scarves, etc.

Strip the three skates down to their blades and platforms. (See the Skate Crow and the Hat for instructions on how to do this, and

SIDE

for ideas for what to do with the uppers.) The main supporting sticks should be the strongest sticks you can find. Fasten them together on the wide edge with lots of 1 1/2" screws. Next make the handle and support section. Cut the stick for the handlebars long enough so that the grip will be at the height of the user's belly button. Brace this handle with a triangle of plywood as shown and two additional struts of stick handle cut at a 45° bevel on each end. Fasten these to the plywood and the shaft with screws or bolts. The lower section of the handle support shaft (B) is connected to the main shaft (A) from underneath and with four additional struts. Now, connect C and D, as shown. This is where you need the nuts and bolts with washers. Cut some small triangular pieces so that the bolts and washers rest at 90° relative to the bolt shaft (see diagram).

Piece A rests on the crosspiece (E). Brace E from above with another triangular plywood piece. There will be a gap between the plywood and E. Use a piece of stick shaft to close this gap and connect the entire joint with nuts and bolts. On the outside edges of E make sure that it is screwed in securely to the skate. This piece must carry the weight of the skater. Most of these skates have a hollow area inside the barrels

DETAIL

that go from platform to blade. Make sure the screw points go through into this spot. Cut another piece of stick that will run the remaining length of the skate. The front of the skate requires a spacer because the heel is higher than the toe. The blades must end up parallel to A, and all skate blades must be in line. Screw the skate, stick and spacer together. Put another couple of screws into the arch area of the skate.

To hold this all together, add a triangular piece of plywood to stabilize the skates. After E is securely installed, add supports (F). Attach the rear skate exactly as you did the front skates. For traction on A wrap a series of grip points with hockey tape.

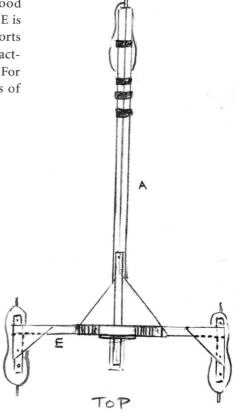

# Over-Reachers:
# Super Long
# Racing Skates

Speed skaters use skates called reachers, with blades that are far longer than hockey skate blades, and they go pretty fast. I figure with these Super Long Skates, baby, you should be doing some low altitude flying.

They don't cost much, either — just a trip down to the Sally Ann and some miscellaneous hardware. Oh yeah, and four broken hockey sticks. Length is really up to you, but I would advise making your first pair no longer than 36" to start learning to skate with these things. Here is what you need to get going: two pairs of old skates, freshly sharpened; six adjustable 6" hose clamps; sixteen 2 1/2" screws; four wood blocks 1" x 2" x 2"; some cardboard for spacing; and your regular skates. Don't worry (he says), this won't mess them up.

Cut your four broken hockey sticks to 36". Next, disassemble the old used skates by cutting the uppers from the skate platform. Do this carefully with a box cutter, using repeated light strokes. The heel will be the biggest problem because of the cardboard reinforcement. Take your time and don't hurt yourself.

When all the blades are free from the uppers, arrange those 1" x 2" x 2" wood blocks as spacers between the skate blades and the stick so that they are horizontal. Now mount your good skates at the mid point of the pairs of sticks, using hose clamps as illustrated, making sure that the skate blades protrude between the sticks. The thicker, rounded part of the skate blade mount should be above the sticks. Put in a cardboard spacer at both ends of the sticks, so that the space between the sticks (the blade width) at the mid point remains consistent all the way along the sticks. Drill pilot holes through the sticks and skate platform so that the screws will end up in the barrels where the blades had been attached to the skate platform. If you're using newer skates with a different support structure, drill into the sturdiest material you can find on that model. When the skate is screwed in through both sticks, in both locations, place a hose clamp around the narrow part of the skate just up from the heel, and tighten it securely.

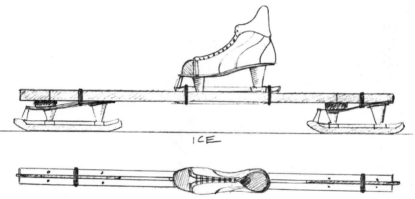

ICE

That about does it for one skate; now make the other. As for using them, go easy the first time — these are honkin' long skates. The good part is that you won't even notice bumpy ice.

# Canadian Rules Cricket

Having reviewed the basics of the game of cricket, I feel that it is time to give this game some ice time. That's right! We need to play cricket in winter as well as in other seasons. To get started, first you have to make the wickets — three vertical posts, called stumps, and two pieces that span these, called bails. Cut three hockey sticks 31" long, allowing 3" to plant the finished stumps into the ice so that your wicket will be the regulation 28" high. Next, cut two 4 1/2" pieces of stick for the bails. Arrange the stumps so that the two on the outside edges are 7" apart and the third is in the centre, creating two equal side-by-side 2 1/2" openings. Then place the bails on top, and your wicket is complete. The bat is simply a goalie stick cut above the curve. You will need two wickets, two bats and a tennis ball to play. Driving the stumps into the ice may present a sticky wicket of a problem. If you prop them up with snow, shorten the stumps accordingly.

Cricket officially calls for two teams of 11 players, but you can decide on any number for a game of shinny cricket. Now the only problem is explaining the rudiments of this game of passion, adored by millions. Believe it or not, cricket may have more fans than hockey has! This isn't the place to describe the finer points of the game, but I'm sure you can find some nerdy pre-teen or old Brit with muttonchops to do that for you. Just install your wickets 22 yards apart and start banging that tennis ball back and forth sometime when there is a crowd around, and you will be amazed at how many expats come forward to tell you you're playing this game wrong. Inform them you are playing Canadian Rules Cricket and get on with it. Hell, make up your own rules. The people who originated the game of cricket did at some point, so you can too.

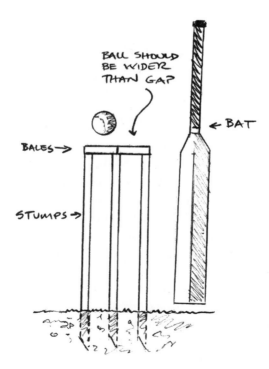

# He Scores! Jumping Guy

HE SHOOTS - SCORES!

NOTE: ILLUSTRATION NOT DRAWN TO SCALE, UNLESS YOU HAVE STICKS ON STEROIDS.

There is true, unbridled joy in a long-awaited goal. Spectators find themselves jumping in celebration, even if they are watching the game on television. But there's a downside to the physical manifestations of this elation. You might spill your beer. The slice of pizza cradled in your lap could easily slide face-down onto the rug. What about the excessive expenditure of valuable calories in jumping up and down? What you really need is a proxy jumper, a wooden figure that rises with arms upraised at your command, with just a slight push of the hand. Now, that's almost as much power as a team owner has, but you don't have to shell out millions for your minion — you just use a broken hockey stick.

This project is pretty involved, so look over the illustrations before you proceed. You will need a scroll saw, a dovetail saw, 3' of abrasion-resistant nylon string, 5 eye hooks, a small hinge 5/8" wide, a length of 3/16" dowel, eight 3/16" internal tooth washers, the blade part of a broken goalie stick, some quick-setting epoxy, and a regular broken hockey stick with about 4' of usable shaft. Look for a stick that is all wood, with no fibreglass or carbon fibre reinforcement. You need to do some fancy cutting, and sticks with those reinforcing components will dull saw blades very quickly. Find a lid from an empty plastic container to mix the epoxy on. Mix it as needed in very small batches as needed.

The jumping and arm-swinging action comes from pushing down on a lever. The arm lines are secured to the base so that, as the figure rises, the arms are pulled upwards. The back of the figure is attached by a hinged bar that allows the figure to slant forwards. The figure sits on a bench with his feet secured to the base. Okay, that's how it works, now let's get started.

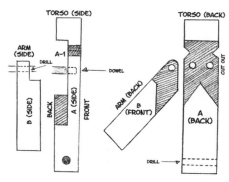

Begin with the torso (A). Cut a length of stick 5" long. Down about 1" from the top of the stick piece, notch out neck grooves about 3/8" in from each side. Cut a 3/8" deep V-shaped lap cut (see illustration) in the back of the torso, so that the notched arms will be flush with the back of the torso, which will allow the arm movement. You can use a scroll saw for the cut from the neck area downwards to the point at which the inverted V shape starts. Then secure the piece in a vise, and make the angular cuts with a dovetail saw.

For the arms (B), cut two pieces of stick 3 3/4" long and round off one end of each so that they will rotate against each other and move freely when installed; a piece of dowel acts as the pivot. Drill with a 3/16" bit through one arm and into the torso in position A-1, without going through the front of the torso. Do the same for the other arm. Cut two pieces of dowel 3/4" long and place one in each hole. This should leave 1/4" of dowel protruding from the back of each arm. Test the rotation of the arms. They should swing freely and not bind. The hole in the arms might need to be routed out more so that they swing freely on the dowel. After reading the instructions and precautions carefully, mix a batch of epoxy about the size of your thumbnail, and place a drop in each hole in the torso. Place the arms on the dowel, and slide a 3/16" internal tooth washer onto the protruding end of the dowel. Put another small dab of epoxy around the washer and the dowel. Be sure to keep epoxy off your skin and clothes. Keep a rag handy to keep tools and hands clean.

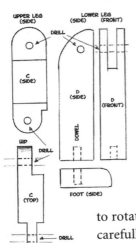

The legs can be cut on a scroll saw. Cut four pieces for the legs: two that are 3 1/4" long for the upper legs (C), and two that are 3 1/2" long for the lower legs (D). Then cut two pieces 1 1/2" long for the feet. Do the cut-outs on the knee joint first, then make the rounded cut at the hip. For the knee joint, cut out the tab first, then do a semicircular cut. The tab should be 1/4" thick. A slot must be cut out of the lower leg. If you use a 1/8" drill bit to make a hole at the interior junction of the cuts, you will be able to rotate the saw blade as you get to each corner. Cut carefully and straight. Do the final rounded cut at the knee end of the lower leg after the slot cut is made.

Drill a hole for the dowel in the centre, 1/2" up from the bottom of the torso. The hole in each upper leg should be at the centre of the curve. At the other end of the upper leg, drill a hole at the centre of the curve. The lower leg is also drilled at the knee joint at the centre of the stick, 3/8" in from the edge. Connect the foot to the bottom of the leg with a piece of dowel epoxied in place.

Put all the pieces together with their respective lengths of dowel and check for ease of movement. Some of the holes might need to be widened a bit so that the limbs swing freely. When everything checks out, use internal tooth washers and epoxy to assemble moving parts.

Now make the bench (E), which should be the height of the seated figure, about 3". Cut two pieces of stick 2 1/4" long for the legs of the bench, and a piece 2 1/2" for the seat. Epoxy or screw this bench together and set aside.

Cut a piece of goalie stick blade 18" long (F). It's okay if part of the shaft is still attached, as long as the whole piece is straight. This will be the base of your creation.

Cut a piece of stick 15" long for the lever (G). Connect it by a hinge to another piece 4" long (I). Connect that to the figure to push him upwards. Epoxy a small block (H) to the top of the lever to stop the hinge from rotating backwards. Every lever needs a fulcrum. Make yours with a piece of stick 3 1/2" wide (J). Drill two holes with a 1/8" bit 1" in from the end and 1/4" down from the top. The fulcrum should be placed 6" from the handle end of the lever. Screw or epoxy the lever in place on the goalie blade. Immediately above the fulcrum, drill a hole with a 3/16" drill bit through the lever.

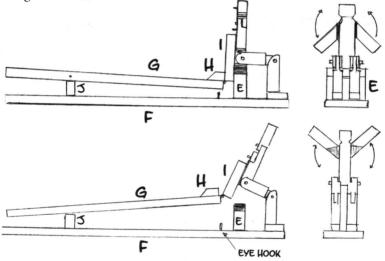

Now you can begin to assemble the whole thing. Place the seated figure on the bench so that the toes of the feet are at the end of the goalie blade. Attach the bench and the feet of the figure to the blade from underneath with screws; drill pilot holes first. Screw the figure to the 4" piece that is part of the lever mechanism. Holding the lever at the fulcrum, push down at the end of the lever and check the figure for ease of movement. Adjust accordingly. Put eye hooks in the backs of the arms, 1" down from the dowel. Put another eye hook in the back of the head. Put two more on either side of the blade base about 1 1/2" back from the bench.

To rig it up, cut two pieces of cord 12" long. Tie off each piece on the eye hooks on the arms. Thread through the eye hook on the head from above and down to the eye hooks on the blade. These lines will need to be tied somewhat loosely. As the figure rises, they will draw the arm lines taut and raise the arms. You want to set them so that, when the figure is as extended as far he will go, his arms are fully upraised. Adjust accordingly.

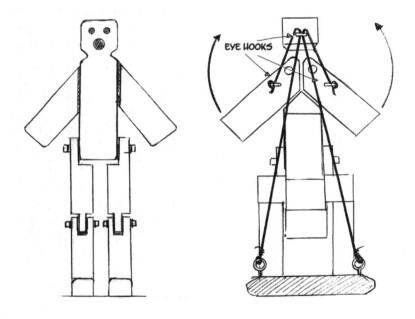

Put a 2" piece of dowel through the lever and attach the lever to the fulcrum with cord. Paint on a face of your choice.

That completes the assembly. Made properly, this action figure should withstand the rigours of many play offs.

# Masks

There has been a tradition of wearing graphically enhanced masks in hockey in recent years, but it's a privilege granted to only one team member, the goalie. In a game between the Montreal Canadiens and the New York Rangers on November 1, 1959, Jacques Plante got a puck in the kisser and needed seven stitches between his upper lip and his nose. Not one to let a trail of blood spoil a game, he donned a flesh-coloured fibreglass face protector and went out to play the rest of the game. Everyone was shocked, but they got over it, we all got over it, and now goalie masks are standard issue. But is this fair? Why can't all team members look wild and crazy? Why can't everyone wear a fabulous mask?

With a mound of hockey junk, you can match goalies in dramatic self-presentation for Halloween or your friendly neighbourhood *ballo in maschera*. You could even turn your own lucky shin pads, your first helmet, and your dad's rotting gloves into a special keepsake to hand down through generations. Surely your descendants will find it worthy of the honour.

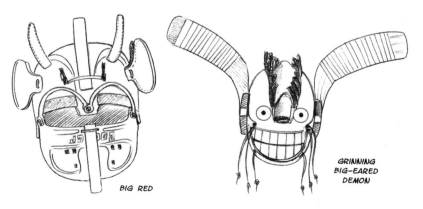

BIG RED

GRINNING
BIG-EARED
DEMON

Masks can be created from a grab bag of equipment: an old elbow pad, felt from your forefathers' padding, a piece of broken stick that once served someone well. The more parts and pieces you can gather, the more striking your mask will be. Go through every bit of equipment that has outlived its usefulness or else just smells too awful to put on again. Cut all the stitched pieces apart with a very sharp X-acto knife, take out the padding, dismember the gloves (especially the older ones with lots of leather), and save everything. Put all the old laces, snaps, ties, and buckles in a shoebox. The only non-hockey equipment I have stooped to include in my own masks are wooden balls, painted to look like eyes, and nylon cable ties, which can be bought in bulk in different sizes. Buy a lot.

Mask creation requires a very special tool, the hot glue gun. In my experience, the yellowish-coloured glue sticks stick better. Also, hot glue works best when it is really hot. This is unfortunate, since the hotter it is, the more it hurts when it gets on your skin. Be careful, and wait until any long, hairlike wisps of hot glue are completely cold before removing them from your mask. To cut up hockey sticks, you will need a saw.

Helmets need to be completely dismantled, that is, stripped down to mere parts, and all the bits of padding, the straps, the buckles, and whatever else is left should be separated into basic components. The more masks you make, the better you'll know helmets, and you'll come to have favourites. For me, Jofa helmets have been the hardest to work with because many are made in one piece. I particularly like Cooper helmets and some of the older CCM models for their great forms. If you can find some old Cooper Weeks helmets, you have really lucked out. They are the best.

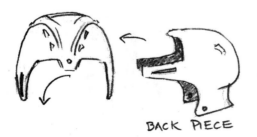

BACK PIECE

FRONT PIECE

A helmet's rigid protective shell usually comes apart in two sections. You might need to explore under the padding to find the screws. Foam padding is usually glued into helmets, and the glue dries out in time, so, with gentle pulling, the padding will come free. You can carve great teeth from some of that old foam, so don't throw it away. Most of the other fasteners in the helmet can be loosened with a screwdriver. Save the cages that protect the face, fasten them together with cable ties, and you'll have a dandy fruit basket or a very coarse colander (see page 89).

The trick with helmet parts is to reassemble them from the shell of the mask into the most mysterious-looking configuration possible. This might mean taking the front piece, turning it upside down, and attaching it to the back of the helmet. The hole created when the helmet parts are joined together will become the mouth, and determining its shape will be an important challenge in finding your mask's character. Some Cooper helmets, when properly reconstituted, produce eye slits similar to those on old European armour. Helmets are so full of holes that you can usually find ways to attach the pieces together with the screws you originally took out, or with cable ties. The attachments need to be secure, with no swivelling parts, unless of course you want them to swivel.

Old leather hockey skates contribute many strange and interesting parts to masks. Remove the leather portion from the base of the skate very carefully with an X-acto knife. Cut along the groove where the leather meets the base of the skate. Don't try to cut through all thicknesses at once, but make several passes of the blade, scoring deeper with each pass. The segment around the heel is particularly tough, but go easy, take your time, and it will come free. To separate the toe section from the rest, slice down between the toe piece and the lower eyelet tab through the stitching. Tongues make great floppy ears, so you should remove the tongue carefully from the toe piece by cutting through the stitching. The leather toe piece, which can be separated from the cardboard toe protector with a bit of effort, will make a particularly good nose.

No two masks will ever be alike, but here's how I made three of my favourites. Once you start imitating the general idea, you'll come up with wonderful designs that no one else on earth could ever imagine.

# Grinning Big-Eared Demon

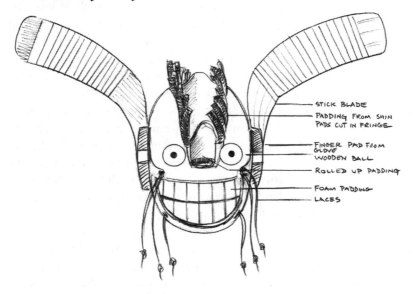

STICK BLADE

PADDING FROM SHIN
PADS CUT IN FRINGE

FINGER PAD FROM
GLOVE
WOODEN BALL
ROLLED UP PADDING

FOAM PADDING
LACES

- 1 CCM PRO STANDARD HELMET
- 2 STICK BLADES
- FELT PADDING FROM AN OLD SHIN GUARD
- FOAM PADDING FROM LEG GUARDS (THE KIND WITH A NYLON COVERING)
- OUTER FINGER PADDING FROM A GLOVE
- FOAM PADDING FROM A HELMET, CUT TO LOOK LIKE TEETH
- 2 WOODEN BALLS
- OLD SKATE LACES
- SCREWS AND CABLE TIES

Remove the foam from the back section of the helmet only. Take the helmet apart, and turn the front section around so that what was once the forehead protector section is now the lower lip. Secure this piece to the other section on the sides of the helmet with some of the screw fasteners you removed when you disassembled the helmet. Cut two stick blades so that

CCM PRO-STANDARD

THIS PIECE IS
FLIPPED

they are of equal length. Just up from the heel, drill two holes in each piece big enough for cable ties to pass through. Fasten these to the side of the helmet with more cable ties. Holes in the helmet might need to be enlarged a bit to accommodate the ties. Do this with a 1/4" drill bit and drill if necessary.

The Mohawk-style "do" is achieved by cutting fringes in the felt of old-style shin pads. This can be taken off the plastic protective shin piece by carefully slicing the stitching with an X-acto knife. Many old shin pads are made of blue felt, which looks distinctive here. Keep the canvas piece attached. Stick the fringe in place with hot glue. The nose is a rolled-up piece of padding from a more contemporary shin pad. Hot glue this in shape and then affix it to the helmet under the canvas piece, again with hot glue. The ear pieces are two finger protectors from an old glove. These can be removed by carefully cutting the stitching with an X-acto knife. Hot glue into position.

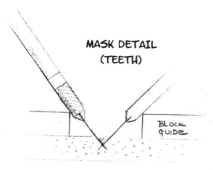

MASK DETAIL
(TEETH)

BLOCK GUIDE

The teeth are cut from foam padding from the helmet. Find a piece that will fill the mouth hole. Using a metal straight edge, rule in teeth shapes with a pencil, and cut along at a 45° angle, 1/8" out from the lines, and then cut towards the lines at the same angle from the other side, again out 1/8". You should be able to cut out long triangular pieces.

When the foam is bent and hot glued in place, it should look like a big rack of teeth. Drill pilot holes in the wooden eyeballs and paint them white. Determine the eye position on the mask, and drill holes there big enough for the screws to pass through. Fasten the balls to the helmet with wood screws. Draw the pupils with a marker or paint. Tie miscellaneous pieces of laces in the remaining holes on the front and under the mask. I tied knots at the ends of these to make them look exotic. If you wish to hang this mask on the wall — and why not? — string some picture hanging wire from holes in the rear of the mask.

# Gator Boy

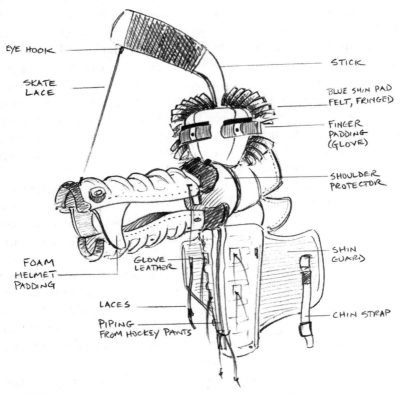

EYE HOOK

SKATE LACE

STICK

BLUE SHIN PAD FELT, FRINGED

FINGER PADDING (GLOVE)

SHOULDER PROTECTOR

SHIN GUARD

FOAM HELMET PADDING

GLOVE LEATHER

LACES

CHIN STRAP

PIPING FROM HOCKEY PANTS

- SHIN PAD (CCM)
- 2 PLASTIC SHIN GUARDS FROM SHIN PADS
  (BACK PADDING AND KNEE PROTECTOR REMOVED,
  LEATHER OR VINYL LEFT ON)
- FOAM PADDING FROM A CCM HELMET
- EXTERIOR FINGER PADDING FROM HOCKEY GLOVES
- SHOULDER PROTECTION PLATE
- OLD SKATE LACES
- BLUE FELT PADDING FROM SHIN PADS
- NYLON PIPING FROM HOCKEY PANTS
- HOCKEY STICK WITH BLADE ATTACHED
- EYE HOOK
- CABLE TIES
- MISCELLANEOUS PIECES

This mask is built on a framework of hockey sticks and held together primarily with cable ties and hot glue. Construct the back bracing with wood screws, as illustrated. Fasten the shin guard to the bracing frame with wood screws. Remove the felt from an old pair of shin pads and cut every 1/4" to make the fringe. Hot glue this to the top of the mask from behind. Remove two pieces of foam finger protectors from an old glove. Hot glue these in position. With a permanent marker, draw eyes where the knuckle delineation is.

For the top jaw, take a plastic shoulder protection plate and drill two holes large enough to accommodate the cable ties near the top, at 10 and 2 o'clock, about 1/2" in from the edge. For the bottom jaw, drill similar holes at 4, 5, 7, and 8 o'clock. Take the shin guards (upper and lower jaws) and put matching holes in the leather or vinyl area that attaches the lower shin guard to the knee cap protector. (Save the upper knee cap piece for other uses.) When attached with cable ties, the upper jaw should hinge upwards and the lower jaw should be stationary. The shoulder protection plate now forms the back of Gator Boy's throat, and if you want to put a face on it, it will look like Gator Boy's last meal.

BACK BRACING

I found some foam padding in a helmet that looked a lot like fangs, but if you have nothing that looks fang-like, cut some foam padding to shape and hot glue to the front of the upper shin guard from the inside. For nostrils, I used pieces of foam, hot glued in place.

The top jaw is supported by a lace tied from an eyehook at the end of the blade of the back brace form. Drill a hole in the centre top at the end of the top jaw and tie a knot in the skate lace to support the jaw. I added bits of palm leather, skate laces and chin guards on the outer fabric as embellishment. I also cut off the piping from a pair of old hockey pants and glued it down the centre of the plastic guard. Picture wire can be attached from behind to hang Gator Boy on the wall.

# Big Red

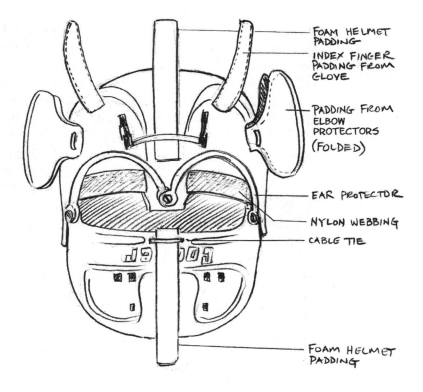

FOAM HELMET PADDING

INDEX FINGER PADDING FROM GLOVE

PADDING FROM ELBOW PROTECTORS (FOLDED)

EAR PROTECTOR

NYLON WEBBING

CABLE TIE

FOAM HELMET PADDING

- COOPER HELMET (SK 2000)
- FOAM PADDING FROM SHOULDER PADS
- OLD HOCKEY GLOVES (LEATHER PREFERABLE)
- PADDING FROM ELBOW GUARDS
- MISCELLANEOUS BITS AND PIECES
- CABLE TIES

This can actually be worn as a mask and has lots of ventilation, although it does kind of stink like an old helmet. Take the helmet completely apart. Turn the front piece so that what once protected the forehead now forms the lower jaw (see illustration on page 64). Attach with available connection pieces removed from helmet. Arrange the pieces that looped onto the chin strap to simulate eyebrows, drill holes in the shell, and attach these pieces at their ends. Cut long pieces from the interior foam to form the crown ridge and jaw ridge. Hot glue these in place, and then secure again with cable ties.

The ear pieces are made from the foam from elbow protectors, folded over and connected with cable ties. The horns are found on the exterior of old hockey gloves between the index finger and the thumb. With an X-acto knife, carefully cut the stitching to remove this piece from each glove, and insert them in suitable ventilation holes where they most approximate horns. I found some old nylon webbing pieces that I hot glued on above the eye holes. To make the back strap that holds the mask on the head, find some Velcro pieces from shin guards and fasten to the back of the helmet with cable ties. Glue some of the remaining foam in place to customize the fit to your face. Add other bits and pieces on the outside of the mask as desired to artfully create your own look.

# Guiro

This instrument, popular in salsa and mariachi bands, is traditionally made out of a gourd with a series of incised grooves. I guess that must be because they don't have many broken hockey sticks in the lands where these instruments were invented. My model uses two pieces of stick and the plastic knee protector from an old shin pad. The only other piece of equipment is a single screw to hold the whole thing together, and the only tool required is a saw — a chop saw would get this project done in no time.

Cut a straight piece of stick 16" long. Mark off the bottom 10" in 1/2" increments. The remaining 6" will be the handle. At the half-inch marks you've made, cut a series of grooves 3/16" wide and about 1/4" deep. Make a hole in the centre of the knee protector, and screw this onto the end of the grooved part of the stick. This will act as the resonator.

Now you need something to play your guiro with. Cut another piece of stick 10" long. Drag the edge of the shorter stick up and down the grooves. Vary the rhythm, using longer and shorter strokes. With a little practice, you'll be the most popular musician at your next kitchen party.

# Lap Steel Guitar

Once upon a time, Lap Steel Guitars were as scarce as auk feathers. They still are. But hockey sticks aren't. It is not too difficult to make this little gem, essential in all open-tuned styles of guitar music. The best thing about this design is that you don't need to worry about the most troublesome aspect of luthierosity. You don't have to lay in metal frets. You might wonder where the expression "quit fretting" came from. Ask a guitar maker. Placing at least 20 pieces of fret wire is fretful work, and screwing it up means that no matter how nicely you did everything else, nobody will want to play your guitar.

With frets out of the way, the rest is simple. Go find an old beat-up electric guitar to use for parts. Try pawn shops, or your local music store will have parts if they do repairs. There is a lively market for old pickups, tuning gears, bridges and volume pods, and many are sold reconditioned and ready to use. The cost of all parts on my guitar came to less than $40, although some old stuff was given to me.

The beauty of this beast is that you just have to do a little bit of bracing, soldering and epoxying. I made my guitar in under three hours. You will need two full-length stick shafts at least 46" long and of a similar make. Epoxy them, blade out, side by side. Be generous with the epoxy, and clamp the two pieces together firmly in several places. This step is like the British secret service: you need a good bond.

On a bought guitar, carefully measure the distance between the "nut" (that's where the strings come over the slotted thing by the tuning pegs) and the bridge. Make a pattern for the frets by cutting a piece of paper the same length as the distance between nut and bridge and marking the positions of the guitar frets. Set this aside for later.

Choose which side of your new guitar will be the top (at this point it doesn't matter) and where the playing area will be. You need about 6" beyond the nut for the tuning pegs. Nut to bridge, your playing area will be about 25". Beyond the bridge, you need about 1 1/2" for the holes through which you'll thread the guitar strings from the back. This whole configuration can be anywhere up and down the stick, as long as the parts are in the right sequence. Measure carefully and mark where the nut and bridge will be from the pattern you made earlier.

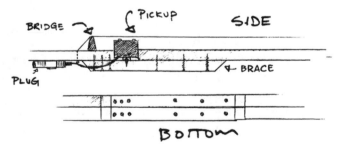

Use the remainder of a stick for the back brace that holds the pickup; it should be about 9" long. For a snazzy appearance, cut the ends of this piece at a 45° angle (see Illustration).

I bought a nut from a local guitar shop, and the guy gave me an old bridge for free. The tuning pegs were also a gift, but they were originally made for nylon strings, so I tune very gingerly and use light-gauge steel strings. The pickup was also thrown my way by somebody else (why do people always throw stuff at me?), and it worked just fine. I test parts like this by wiring the pickup to a 1/4" mono plug and patch that into a guitar amplifier. If they don't buzz but still pop when you tap the pickup, they probably work fine.

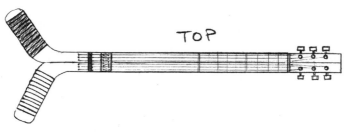

TOP

You will need to chop-cut the stick to form a slot in which to nestle the pickup, and therefore you must add a brace on the back side. I have illustrated this so expertly that it is perfectly clear to everyone. The important thing to remember is that you must have enough overlap to withstand the stress of the strings. I used six screws on each side, and my guitar seems to be holding up fine. Of course, use screws that are shorter than the combined thickness of the sticks. If you have the gizmo to recess the screw heads, use it so the heads won't catch on your clothes when you have the guitar on your lap.

The placement of the pickup in relation to the bridge changes the tone. Move it closer to the bridge for a brighter (treble) sound, and move it farther away for more bass. Guitars like the Fender Stratocaster have three different pickups installed to give good tone selection. I put my pickup about 3" from the bridge, and it sounds pretty good to my abused ears.

The tuning pegs come in many forms. Depending on what you get, replicate the arrangement on the tuning end of your new instrument. This will most likely involve drilling through the sticks. Avoid drilling where the sticks are joined with epoxy. On some guitars, the strings go under a piece between the nut and the tuners. This piece applies tension downwards, keeping the strings in the grooves of the nut in case you strum very energetically. Any metal bar can work for this. I found a piece from a broken scooter that worked, but you might want to look around at guitars to see the shape to look for.

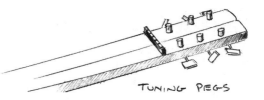

TUNING PEGS

The wiring up of the pickup to the plug is not a big deal. Some pickups just have two wires, and others have two wires per pickup group and a ground. Trial and error will tell you which wires go where. Remember your rules of electricity: there is a positive, a negative and a ground. If your amplifier is in order, there should be no risk of electrical shock. Attach wires with the power off. A loud buzzing when the power is on means you should try another arrangement, such as putting similar coloured wires together. When all is figured out, solder the connections. If you are not familiar with soldering, ask for assistance. Should you also want to install the tone and volume pods, the wiring gets trickier. If you are taking these elements off an existing guitar, make good notes as to what goes where. These controls can be placed on the outer blade of the lap steel guitar. Use hockey tape to secure all loose wires and perhaps even the 1/4" plug receptor.

Now, using the pattern for where the frets go, paint, draw, or use thin tape to demarcate fret positions. As you get the hang of this guitar, you will notice that the 5th, 7th and 12th frets are the most important. The 12th fret position should be the octave. Make these lines stand out from the others for quick visual reference while you are playing.

Once assembled, the instrument can be tuned conventionally (EADGBE), or tuned "open," like a chord. I play my guitar to an "E" tuning with an old socket spark plug wrench. Holding the piece perpendicular to open-tuned strings creates a chord no matter where you place it. Try sliding the metal piece up and down the neck. Sliding up the neck towards the pickup will give you a sound like the early Looney Tunes intro music. Conventional tuning requires a working knowledge of where notes are on the neck. Playing any instrument well requires practice, so your virtuosity lies in your discipline. This guitar will work and sound so great that you'll have to do as I did: start a "stick" band.

# Electric Guitar

ood guitarists are always being complimented about their "stick handling." So, if your old hockey stick gets too heavily handled, turn it into an electric guitar. It's way easier than you think. I found an old guitar neck at a pawn shop, with tuning pegs still attached. This made irrelevant the pesky fret and neck issue of guitar making. I just needed to make a guitar body out of hockey sticks.

I laminated two 11" pieces of hockey stick along the thinner side to make a piece about 2 1/4" wide. Guitar necks have mounting hardware, so I used an awl to mark exactly where pilot holes should be, drilled the pilot holes, and attached the neck to one end of the laminated sticks.

In searching for the right bridge, you will probably come across an old "whammy bar" model. This is an excellent source for a bridge that is right at the end of the guitar, and you'll have a very portable and compact instrument. Depending on your choice of bridge, you might have to mount it on another piece of hockey stick added crossways at the end of the guitar. Cut this piece wider and you can also attach the blades that form the body of the guitar (see next page). Mount whatever pickup you are using down near the bridge, so the sensors are not more than 1/8" away from the strings.

Here's a quick lesson in electrodynamics. A guitar pickup works by vibrating a metal string over a magnetic field. Unplayed, the guitar makes no sound, but pluck a string and you have created an impulse. This impulse is a slight electric current that is sent down the line to the amplifier. The closer the guitar string to the pickup, the stronger the signal. The closer the pickup to the bridge, the brighter the sound. This has to do with wave forms in the vibrating string. Harmonic points of a vibrating string (pivot points along a series of sine waves) are easy to find at the half- and quarter-points along the string. The closer the pickup is to these points, the mellower the sound. A rock guitarist playing lead wants a bright, penetrating tone and therefore uses a pickup away from the harmonic points and close to the bridge.

Before you attach the pick-up permanently to your new guitar, experiment with placement to get the sound you like best. If you have a few sets of pickups, position them like the pickups on a guitar whose sound you like. Look closely at how these are wired together, and take good notes so you can install them on your guitar. Some mounting holes are wider apart than the sticks you laminated together. If that's the case, make a mounting plate from a piece of 1/4" plywood. You might have to shim up the pickup so that it is close to the metal strings.

Wire the pickup and guitar plug receptor on the back of the guitar. Solder all connections. Use hockey tape to keep wires from getting jostled. Since I chose not to hook up the tone and volume knobs on my version but adjust the volume with the amplifier, I have a pretty simple set-up. If you wish to play standing up, add the knobs that will attach to a guitar strap, one at the heel of the guitar and the other where the neck meets the body.

If you quit at this point, you'll have a very skinny guitar, worthy of true stick handling. Or you can add some body to it. I used two stick blades, cut so that they would lie almost parallel to the neck. These could be flared out, however, for a more "flying V" look. Epoxy the blades to the body sticks and attach them with screws to the crosspiece that the bridge rests on. You will find this a very light instrument and very playable, but you will have to share it, as many others will wish to play it, too. This is the guitar to bring to wild parties because it stands up to abuse so well.

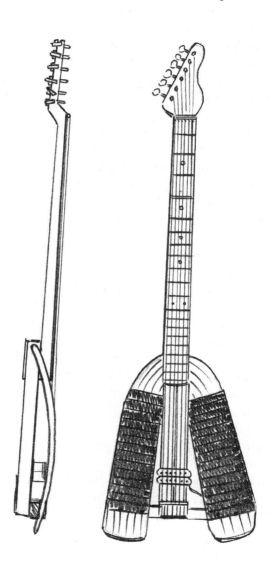

# Castanet Sticks

The Maritime kitchen party band often has an improvised percussion component. Sometimes it is the beat that is being improvised, and sometimes the improvisation is in grabbing the nearest implement and banging it on something in a rhythm somewhat close to that of the song being played. Nothing is precise in the cloud of late night spirits. Often, someone will hold a pair of spoons loosely between the fingers and slap them between the palm and the thigh. Spoons are similar to the instrument the Irish call "bones," which is truly devilish to master. Irish bones used to be made of pigs' ribs, but I prefer wooden ones with a similar rib shape. I have devised a musical instrument that is a combination of spoons and bones, a clapper that gives a sharp castanet-like sound and is a no-brainer to play.

It is comprised of two pieces of hockey stick, cut to the same length, a piece of foam padding from a hockey glove, and a skate lace. The only tools required are a drill with a 1/4" bit and a saw.

The sticks can be any size between 6" and 18" long — the longer the stick, the deeper the tone. As long as you are making one set of castanet sticks, you might as well make a few of them, all in different sizes. A semicircle of these clappers can draw the attention away from those bothersome fiddle players to the rhythm section, the true heart of any jam session.

Once stick size has been determined and the sticks cut, use the 1/4" bit to drill a hole 3/4" down from the end of each stick. Next, choose the foam you will use — the kind I prefer is found in the band that goes around the back of the wrist on the exterior of hockey gloves, usually sewn into a fabric tube. The older Cooper gloves have two foam pieces 1/2" x 1 3/16" x 5". Cut one piece 1 1/2" long and make a hole in it 3/4" from the end. Place the foam insert between the two sticks, lining up the holes. To assemble your castanet sticks, double the skate lace and tie a knot 10" from the tipped ends. Thread the two tips up through the bottom stick, the foam and the top stick. Pull the doubled lace tight until the knot you made slides up against the hole in the bottom stick. Loop the laces back down around the sides of the clapper and tie securely over the hole where the laces were first inserted.

The castanet sticks are best played sitting down, clapping them between the top of the thigh and
the palm of the hand.

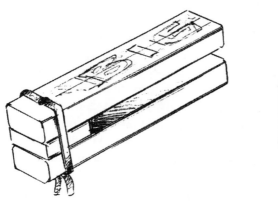

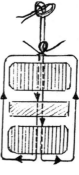

# Timbales

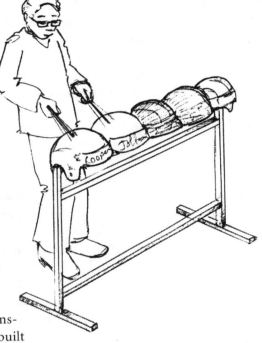

**W**ouldn't you love to have a set of drums made of old hockey helmets? This design was created by the well-known percussionist Shawn Bostick — well known in Sackville, New Brunswick, at least. Shawn built himself a hockey stick marimba and added this innovative helmet drum feature. Shawn and I have performed with the Stick Band, made up mostly of hockey stick instruments, for no less a hockey legend than the great Frank Mahovlich himself.

To construct this set of *timbales*, which I think means numbskull in Spanish, you will need a saw, a drill, at least a dozen L brackets and screws, at least six hockey sticks in reasonable shape, a length of wooden dowel, and five hockey helmets — different coloured ones will result in a more striking look. If you remove all the padding, and strike the helmets with a purchased drumstick, you will hear that each model has a different tone, which can be adjusted by removing various pieces of the helmets.

Start by measuring the combined width of all the helmets you will be using. The drum kit will be 3" wider than that, so cut the top crosspiece, which will hold the helmets, to that total length. Cut two more crosspieces 1 1/2" shorter than the top crosspiece. The height of the stand itself is relative to the height of the user. The tops of the helmets should be about level with the drummer's belly button. So measure that height and then cut two hockey sticks to that length to serve as the uprights of the *timbales* stand. Then cut two stick pieces long enough to stabilize the uprights, and attach one to the bottom of the uprights with L brackets and screws. You can beef this up easily with additional brackets, should you be planning on really pounding your drums. These can be added as sections of hockey stick cut at 45° angles at each end and fastened to the bottom and upright pieces. The second crosspiece goes near the top of the uprights, and it can be either screwed on or mounted with L brackets. A combination of the two would make the stand extra strong for those really vigorous jam sessions. Once the uprights are stabilized, drill a hole and insert a length of dowel into the exposed ends, creating a holder for the drum section.

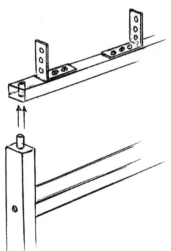

At each end of the longer crosspiece, the one that will hold the helmets, drill holes big enough to accommodate the exposed dowels. Use wood screws to attach L brackets to the crosspiece, spaced so that an L bracket fits inside the first and last helmet on the crosspiece, as well as sandwiched between where the helmets meet side-by-side. This will require six L brackets across the top. Then bolt the helmets to L brackets so that the tops of them are all level. This might mean drilling extra holes in the helmets so that they line up. If the helmets don't feel solid, tighten them up by screwing them directly together near the L brackets with additional wood screws. Finally, pop the drum section onto the stand. When finished, you might polish the helmets up a bit so that they look flashy. Oh yeah, if you are a beginner, buy a metronome and start practising.

# Umbrella

**T**his umbrella could come in handy in all seasons, even indoors. Believe it or not, some hockey rinks are in crummy buildings that leak like sieves when it rains. You would think that our temples to ice (honouring the goddess Isis, I understand) would be pristine constructions, without leaks, foul smells or splintery seats. Ah, but that would come under the heading "perfect world."

You can make an umbrella from hockey sticks using just a few tools. You will need a saw capable of making box joints, a coping saw or scroll saw, a drill with a 1/4" bit, and a sewing machine. To connect this contraption together you will require: bolts with nuts and washers (two 3 1/2", two 3", and four 1 1/4"); four 6" lengths of 1/4" nylon cord, and some lighter string to tie the canopy to the spars (canopy supports); a sturdy eye hook; and four 1" wood screws. You'll need five hockey sticks in all. The blades don't have to be on, though they'd add a nice touch. I suggest you use all-wood sticks for everything but the main shaft. Some quick-setting epoxy is required for the sliding collar piece. The canopy size depends on the length of stick used. The directions for this model are based on 30" long spars. You will need some sturdy waterproof fabric — enough to cut four triangular pieces with at least a 1/2" seam allowance on all sides. If your fabric is 36" wide, for example, you will need to purchase 2 yards to give you the 4 triangles you need.

The shaft stick (B), which could be fibreglass-reinforced, should be at least 40" long. Like any umbrella, this one needs a sliding mechanism that goes up the shaft to allow it to open and close. Make this with four 5" pieces of hockey stick. Drill holes for the connecting bolts through the

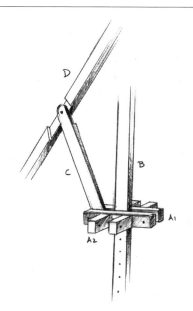

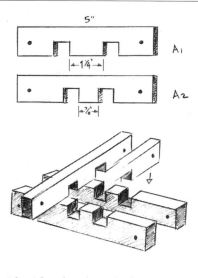

wide side of each end of each piece. There are two box cuts per piece, cut to the mid point of the wide side of the sticks. Two of these pieces are notched against the wide side of the shaft stick (1 1/4") and the other two are notched against the narrow side of the shaft stick (7/8", see A1 and A2). These interlock to form the collar that the struts attach to. Assemble the collar pieces, check for fit so that the collar slides smoothly up the shaft stick. If all is A-OK, epoxy these four pieces in place, making sure that no drips go into the centre.

Now cut four struts (C), 12" long, square at one end. The other end is cut to accommodate the rotation where it connects with the spar (D). Make the diagonal box cut across the wide side of the stick, 2" down from the end at a 45° angle. This should leave about 3" on the other side. Place the stick in a vise, and cut down the centre of the narrow side to complete the mortise.

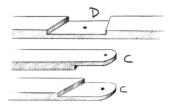

There are four spars, part D, each 30" long. Cut the butt end at a 30° angle. Leave the blade on the other end if you like, or cut that end square (90°). Drill holes through the pointed ends, which will rest at the top of the umbrella, to accommodate the cord that will attach to the shaft. Ten inches down from the point of each spar, make the lap cut that will join it to the strut (C). This is a cut at 90° at the top and 45° at the bottom. The cut is 2 1/2" wide on one side and 3 1/2" on the other, cut to the mid-point of the stick (a 3/8" recess). Drill a hole in the centre of this cutout for bolting each spar to C.

Screw the eye hook into the top of the shaft stick. Loop pieces of cord through the holes you drilled in the spars (D), and tie them to the eye hook, so that they all hang equally. Bolt the spars to the struts (D to C), using the 3 1/2" and 3" bolts, and then to their respective slots on the movable collar (A), using the 1/14" bolts. Check for movement and action. If the collar binds on the shaft, try applying a little soap as a lubricant. Take measurements of the four spaces where the fabric will form the canopy. Add a 1/2" seam allowance to each side, then cut and sew the fabric pieces together. Sew in a loop of string at the outside edge of all the seams to attach the canopy to the spars. Drill a hole in each spar at the point where fabric ends. and tie the loop to the spar.

Select an item (such as a nail with its point filed down) to use as a set pin to hold the sliding collar in place. Drill a series of holes, slightly larger than your set pin, at 2" intervals along the shaft stick. Open the umbrella, choose how stretched you want it to be, slide the pin through the appropriate hole, and there you are: safe from any element that should happen by.

Should your umbrella need a longer shaft for planting in the sand or snow, screw another length of hockey stick, blade removed, to the bottom of the shaft, leaving the collar movement unhindered. You are now the proud owner of a hockey stick umbrella, which I am sure will be admired by all who witness its splendour.

# Skate Hat

**H**ere is a quick and easy fashion statement. All you need is an old leather skate. The saying about silk purses and sows' ears applies to this project because you will be the object of veneration when you wear this *chapeau de patin*.

Cut the leather off the skate base very carefully. Use a sharp X-acto knife to cut just above where the base material attaches to the leather. Make multiple light passes along the cut rather than trying to cut through the whole thickness all at once. You can injure yourself that way. The heel will give you the most trouble, but be patient and it will come off. Cut the connection at the toe piece through the stitching from the inside seam. Once the leather is freed from the skate, run the lace through the first few eyelets closest to the toe.

The upper part of the skate that used to form the ankle support is now the visor. Put on that hat and go to town. Make another hat for your buddy with the other skate.

# Your
# Very Own
# Supermodel

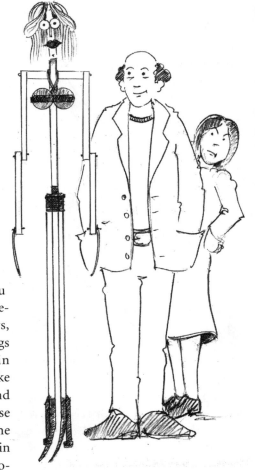

**Y**ou have seen super-
models on TV and at
the supermarket check-
out — that place where you
check out the odd celebrity be-
haviour on magazine covers,
you check out the many bags
of junk food in the cart in
front of you, and then you take
your cheque out, only to find
out that they don't take those
any more. But back to the
babes . . . if you have blood in
your veins and XY chromo-
somes, the idea of dating one of those slim, slinky beauties might have
crossed your mind. I'll tell you one thing, a date with your own
homemade supermodel won't cost you a mint. This model won't eat
much of that expensive caviar you dished up on her plate, and she's a very
moderate drinker.

Now, you don't see too many real live supermodels at hockey games.
This could be attributed to a couple of factors. First, there is so little meat
on their bones that they just can't stay warm, even if they wear one of
those poofy jackets to the rink. The second reason for their scarcity at the

local arena is their fear that you might not be able to discern the difference between them and the hockey sticks. Both are quite slim, and believe it or not, although a supermodel can't be turned in to a hockey stick, some sticks can be turned into a supermodel. These ladies are tall, so choose sticks accordingly.

Here is what you need to put your supermodel together: five hockey sticks, two of them with blades still attached; two hockey pucks in lieu of bosomy silicone implants; some hockey tape; two 1 1/4" wooden balls for eyes; a string mop head for hair; and bits and pieces cut from stick blades for face and hand parts. This figure is articulated (if not articulate), so you'll need some wood screws or nuts and bolts to hold it all together. Tools required are a drill and bits for drilling pilot holes for screws or bolts, a coping saw or scroll saw for the tricky cuts, and a regular chop saw for the square cuts. To stick parts together, you will need some quick-setting epoxy or a hot glue gun.

Build this babe from the ground up: start with some extreme heels. Take the two sticks with the blades still intact, and cut the blades into long, spiky shoe shapes. The heels are the handle ends from two other sticks, cut at a 45° angle and screwed to the leg shaft from the outside. To keep this fashion statement on track, use black hockey tape to wrap the heel and shoe of each foot.

Chiropractors tell us that we all have one leg shorter than the other, and now I'm telling you, too. So, cut one of the sticks with the feet attached 2" shorter than the other. My supermodel, for example, has one 40" leg and one 38" leg. This gives her a provocative pose, with one leg thrust forward when she's standing. No need for knees here. A beauty like this will always have some guy around to pick up anything she drops.

FOOT

Next cut the torso piece 24" long. Bolt the legs to the torso, and when they're properly tightened, wrap this area with hockey tape to simulate a very tiny miniskirt. Next, 16" up from the skirt, tape on two hockey pucks, being creative in the wrapping and strapping. This is *bas couture*, pal, so really go for it. Next, cut a piece of stick 7" long for the shoulders. Screw this piece on from behind, 3" down from the top. The arms are built with three pieces of stick. The upper arm and forearm are each cut

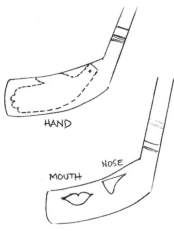

HAND

NOSE

MOUTH

12" long. The wrists and hands are shaped from hockey stick blades, one left and one right, so that the hands turn inward and look hand-like when completed. Build the arms so that the upper arms bolt to the shoulders, the forearms bolt to the outsides of the upper arms, and the hands bolt to the outsides of the forearms.

The head is a 7 1/2" piece of hockey stick with a 3" piece screwed to the top to hold the mop/wig/hair. The head-piece is screwed to the front of the torso piece, so that the head is askew in a coquettish sort of way. With a scroll saw or a coping saw, cut the lips and nose shapes from hockey stick blades. To attach the lips, first drive a screw into the appropriate spot and let it protrude 1" from the stick. Glue the lips to the protruding screw head, then glue the nose just above that. Paint the 1 1/4" wooden balls that you'll use to make the eyes. Glue the eyes to-gether, or, if you feel up to a bit of a challenge, drill holes in the eyeballs for wooden dowels and insert the dowels, making them secure with glue. The eyeballs should be touching each other. When these are assembled, glue them to the head. You might experiment with pupil placement for the proper ex-pression. Did she have too much Dom Perignon? Is she surprised at your home decor? Is she dazed by countless days in Capri? You're the boss in this de-partment. Finally, carefully drape the string mop over the top piece and glue it along the fabric strip

EYE
OPTIONS

you'll find inside it. Style this hair to your taste. Try to keep the hair out of the face, but leave a few errant strands in front for that studied dishev-elled look.

This model, when completed, will never dump you for the team hunk. No, she will lean gracefully forever against the wall of your room.

# Baskets

ere's the scenario: It is Mother's Day, St. Valentine's Day, St. Patrick's Day, a birthday, or any day when a gift is in order, and like a big uncaring slob, you don't have a stinking thing to show your appreciation, love, or both. You are broke and the stores are closed anyway. You do, however, have a basement full of old hockey stuff. Chances are getting better that you just might be able to come up with something after all!

# Carrying Basket / Fruit Basket

**W**hat you need for this basket are two old face guards. The plastic ones won't work here, you need the metal ones. Remove the two screws that normally hinge the face guards to the front of the helmet. Unbend and remove the two metal pieces. If your helmets are both the same brand, well, then, their face guards will match. If not, all praise for asymmetry. I found a Cooper and a Joffa. The Cooper has an extension of sorts that could serve as a handle, although it is a little off centre.

Plastic cable ties work best to attach the two face guards to each other. Strap the two pieces together in at least three places and trim off the excess cable tie just beyond where it loops through the face guard. If you do not have cable ties, use wire or string and tie it carefully, taking the time to make beautiful knots.

If your gift is to be a fruit basket, you are done. If you want to make it into a carrying basket, find an old leather belt, thread it through the top rungs of the face guards at the centre, and buckle it to form the handle. Paint if only if absolutely necessary. Incidentally, I have found that this whole arrangement could be used as an umpire's face guard if you add a little padding.

# Pantry Basket

To make one of those hanging basket sets that hold the onions, potatoes and whatnot in your pantry, all you have to do is follow the assembly instructions for the fruit basket, make as many as you need, and use shoelaces to string them together in a series. Skate laces might be long enough to hang three baskets in a row. Use at least three laces spaced evenly around the perimeter of the baskets for proper balance. I made one of these for an "in" basket for my fan mail. Oddly enough, it's empty.

# Bread Basket

Find a two-piece helmet (like a Cooper SK600) and remove all the interior padding. Unscrew the face guard, ear protectors and chin strap. You should reduce the entire helmet to just the two plastic pieces held together by screws. This particular style of helmet makes a good container because it won't tip. Run it through the dishwasher to make sure it is nice and clean before using it. If you are using this basket for a formal meal, resist using an old hockey jersey for a liner and find a clean napkin or tea towel.

# Tents

In those merciful few weeks of Canadian summer, we dare to venture to the beaches to soak up a little vitamin D and a couple of brews. You can provide a bit of shade by making a tent out of a few hockey sticks and some old tarp material. Should you care to splurge on fabric, a colourful lightweight nylon would make these tents quite attractive.

Models 1 and 2 disassemble easily and can be stowed in a canoe, and Model 2 could be rigged for a shady downwind ride in said canoe, as long as it is placed so that the person steering the craft can see without obstruction. The upscale Model 3 is more involved and requires 12 sticks — a whole team's worth.

TENT
MODEL 2

# Tent Model 1

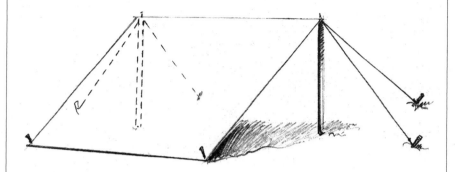

This is the basic model. Use a tarp 8' wide and 6' long, with grommets at the four corners. Cut two sticks 36" long for the tent poles, and drive a nail halfway down into one end of each. Then, cut up another stick or two into six stakes that are 12" long, square on one end, and pointed on the other. You will need four 8' lengths of cord for the front and side tension cords, and two shorter lengths to attach to the two back stakes. Drive the two back corner stakes into the ground, and attach them to the back corner grommets of the tarp with the shorter pieces of cord. Insert the tall tent poles into the front corner grommets, and loop the ends of two of the 8' cords around the protruding nail in the end of each tent pole. Stake the loose ends into the ground and then adjust the tension to make your tent taut. This is a time-tested design for camping, canoeing, or hanging out at the beach.

# Tent Model 2

**M**odel 2 (also see illustration on page 92) will provide wind protection and, depending on how you set it up, some sun protection. It easily disassembles into a very portable roll. You'll need to do some sewing and installing of grommets. You'll need four 2" long bolts and wing nuts, four wood screws with wide heads, two nails and two pieces of stick cut into stakes to hold the support lines. The grommet holes should be bigger than the nail heads but smaller than the screw heads.

The size of this tent depends on the size of the available sticks. A personal-sized shelter would require two 30" long sticks and two that are 36" long. Drill holes in the wide side at both ends of each stick to accommodate connecting bolts. The fabric is 38" wide and 90" long, allowing for 1/2" seams. The "wings" would then be 36" long along the ground with a grommet at the point. My basic math would make the hypotenuse 44" long. Set up the rectangular frame with bolts and wing nuts. Cut a triangle 37" long and 38" wide from the fabric and sew to the other end, as illustrated, with 1/2" seams on all edges.

After the fabric is sewn, place the stick frame over the rectangular area of the fabric. Stretch the fabric over the frame, and make four marks in each corner where the bolts are located in the frame. Install a grommet at these points. The bolts can now be placed through the grommets and two

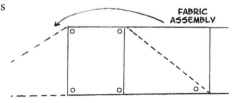

FABRIC
ASSEMBLY

pieces of hockey stick at each corner and fastened with a wing nut. The crosspieces can then be taken off from the inside by unscrewing the wing nuts, so the whole rig can be rolled up. At the top of each 36" piece, hammer in a nail leaving the head protruding 1/2". Attach the supporting lines to the nail heads, and stake these lines behind the shelter. These two supporting cords are 8' long, and the stakes should be cut 12" long, with one pointed end. You can adjust the angle of the frame with the support lines and the spread of the wings with the stakes. On a really windy day, you might consider adding extra stakes at the bottom of the frame, attaching them to the tent with loops of cord tied to the bottom corners.

# Tent Model 3

Fancy camping goods stores charge hundreds of dollars for things like high-tech tarps, but you can make an entire shelter for what you'd pay in taxes on that tarp, as long as you have lots of broken hockey sticks. It won't be quite as light as the fancy-schmancy model that costs a fortune, but if you can haul around a full hockey gear bag for months during hockey season, lugging this tent will be nothing. The added benefit of this model is that either end could be the opening — just rock the tent to the other side. This innovation is a tremendous bonus when the wind is quirky.

The strength of this model is in the four triangulations. Since there are three sticks joining at six points, and four coming together at the remaining two points, there are also many very weird angles involved. I have made life easy for you by suggesting the use of nylon cord to hold these points together. By threading cord through holes in the sticks and tying it securely, you will also have the advantage of a flexible structure. We all want flex at the beach, especially if it is a muscle beach.

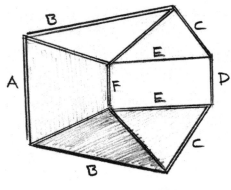

**BIRD'S-EYE VIEW**

I have designed this model on the assumption that the longest hockey stick handle available is 48". Start with cutting six stick pieces 36" long (B). They form two equilateral triangles, one for each side of the tent. Next cut A, 30" long; F, 16" long; and D, 16" long. Piece C is the longest at 48", and E is 36" long. Since you will be securing all the ends with cord, you can make all the cuts square (90°). Drill holes in both ends of all pieces, large enough to accommodate the cord you are using. You will need eight pieces of cord 12" long for connectors. If you choose nylon cord, singe the ends so that they won't unravel with use.

Loosely tie the six 36" B pieces into two triangles. Then tie one 30" piece (A) between the two triangles, then add F, with E, D and C following sequentially. When all pieces are connected, go back to each joint and tie the cord as tightly as possible. The fabric covering will give the structure more strength when it is on the frame. Believe it or not, making this covering is really not that difficult. If your structure is just meant to provide protection from bugs, you can simply drape a mosquito net over the whole thing. But, for more protection, purchase a 12' x 12' piece of utility tarp, which will be large enough to hang over the frame.

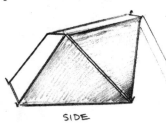

An unmotivated sort would just creatively duct tape everything in place.

A more ambitious soul would sew it all together. Please make sure to use a heavy-duty machine that is capable of sewing heavy-duty tarp material. Here is what worked for my struc-

SIDE

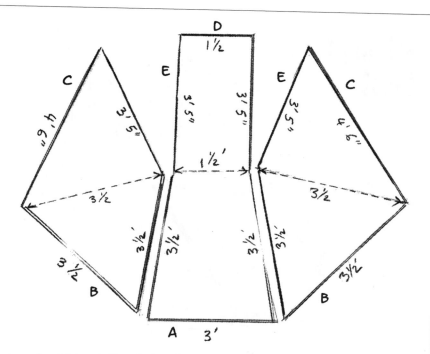

ture. I cut triangle B and the adjacent triangle C as one panel, and made a duplicate of that for the other side of the tent. Then I cut and sewed the back section (A-F) and top (F-D) for the third panel. I used the frames for measurements and added 1/2" on all sides for the seam allowance. I added a grommet at each outside corner once the tarp panels were sewn together. Then I put loops of cord through each of these for tying off to stakes.

Before taking the whole thing apart, don't forget to label each piece clearly with a permanent marker so you can put it together correctly the next time without losing your sanity.

FRONT

# Folding Camp Stool

T his stool can be put together in short order. It can be used for hanging out around the campfire or as a seat for landscape painters. It is very similar to the one used by A.Y. Jackson in his painting days, when folks would ask, "Why you painting that for, eh? Why, Jackson?" He loved this type of stool because it allowed him to turn around quickly and keep on painting, ignoring the queries.

This stool requires several different lengths of hockey stick pieces, so measure accurately when you are making your cuts. You'll need four pieces 18" long, two pieces 11" long, two 13 1/2" long pieces, and, finally, four 2" long pieces. Also, you'll need a bit of hardware: ten screws 2 1/4" long, eight 1 1/4" screws, and two bolts 2 1/2" long with washers and nuts, as well as twenty #3 upholstery tacks. You will need a piece of canvas or other sturdy cloth 20" x 23". Tools required are a hammer, drill and saw, plus a sewing machine and an iron.

First, make the seat. Lay the piece of canvas out flat and fold it in half, so that you end up with a piece that is 11 1/2" x 20". Use the sewing machine to stitch a seam 1/2" in from the long edge, opposite the fold. Turn what is now a sleeve inside out, and iron the edges flat. Strengthen the fabric by sewing three more seams lengthwise down the middle at 1/4" intervals, then turn the fabric sideways and repeat the seam pattern. Next, centre the fabric on the wide side of one each of the 11" and the 13 1/2" hockey stick pieces, and tack it in place using the upholstery tacks, ten on each stick. If you are using hockey sticks with fibreglass reinforcement, use an awl to start the tack holes and then hammer them in. Be sure to do this on a worktable and not on your lap. An awl leaves a very painful hole in your body if it slips.

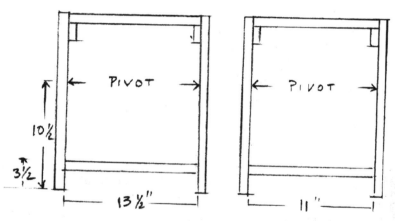

Now you are ready to make the legs. Drill pivot point holes, large enough for the 2" long bolts to thread through, in the four 18" stick pieces, just slightly above the centre point for proper balance. With legs of this length, the holes should be 10 1/2" from the bottom. The remaining 13 1/2" and 11" stick pieces form the lower leg braces. Screw them in place against the inside of the wide side of each of two pairs of legs, 3 1/2" from the bottom of each leg. Notice that one frame is wider than the other. That is so that the narrow frame can pivot inside the wide one when the stool is folded. Place the narrow frame inside the wide frame, lining up the drilled holes. Thread the bolt heads through from the outside, washer and nuts on the inside.

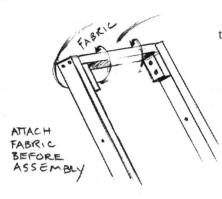

ATTACH
FABRIC
BEFORE
ASSEMBLY

Assemble the stool according to the diagram. Wind the fabric on both sticks one full turn, so that the fabric is wrapped around the stick and the tacks are facing upwards. Then attach each end of the seat assembly to the inside of the top of the legs. Now drill pilot holes in each of the four 2" stick pieces. Place the 2" stick pieces at the inside top of each leg, where the seat meets the frame, and screw them snugly in place against the seat fabric, using the 1 1/4" screws.

TACKS ON THIS EDGE

Do some light sanding on the legs, and if there are fibreglass threads present, wrap the leg end with hockey tape.

This design is easily changeable to make a taller stool or shorter stool — just adjust the leg length to suit your fancy.

# Stealth Grabber

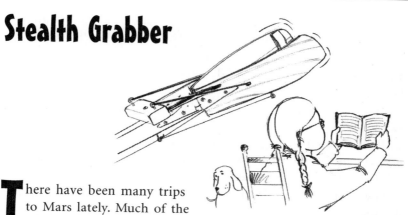

There have been many trips to Mars lately. Much of the hoopla is actually about the ability to pick stuff up once the spacecraft gets there. I have had open access to the schematic plans for those dirt grabber things that they send to the Red Planet, and I have recreated one here with absolute attention to detail. Well, granted, they don't use hockey sticks a whole lot in space exploration. They spend gazillions of dollars creating something that is not even as well-engineered as a good hockey stick, and then it doesn't work!

To make such a contraption that does work, you'll need string, two 3" strap hinges, two rubber bands, eight eye hooks, a length of handle from a broken hockey stick, some padding from an old helmet, two regular stick blades (one left and one right), and a piece of goalie stick blade.

The successful pincher/grabber device has good leverage. To achieve this, you need a piece of stick about 5" long. Mount it on its wide side to the thin side of the length of stick that will be the grabber's shaft, 2" from the end. Attach this crosspiece with two screws so that it won't twist. Place eye hooks on the top at each end of this piece. Attach a strap hinge onto each wide side of the shaft, so that the hinge is right at the end and opens out away from the shaft. Now screw the open side of each hinge to a hockey stick blade so that both blades curve inward and their tips face each other. The screws

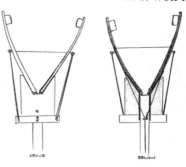

ABOVE          BELOW

that come with the hinges might be longer than the blades are thick. In that case, use appropriately sized nuts and bolts, or file off the points of the screws once they are secure. This is a real pain, so I would advise the nuts and bolts approach, although I did enjoy the sparks shooting from my Dremel tool.

Once you've secured the blades to the hinges, you will notice that they swing widely. You need to rein in those blades. So, get a piece of goalie stick blade about 4" long, and cut a V shape along the wide side of the blade about 2" deep. Attach this with one screw to the stick so that its flat side butts right up against the crosspiece.

Now comes the riggin'. Put in one eye hook about 1" beyond the tip of the hinge on the outside of each blade. Halfway up on the bottom of each blade, put in another eye hook. Put another eye hook on the bottom of the shaft directly beneath the crosspiece, and another about 30" down from that. You could add more eye hooks so that the arrangement starts to look like a fishing rod. Find a length of abrasion-resistant string more than 60" long. Tie one end to the eye hook under the crosspiece and loop it through the eye hook on the lower right side of the blade, through to the other lower eye hook opposite that one, back through the eye hook with the knot on it, and through the final eye hook at the handle end. Tie a piece of hockey stick to this end of the string so it will stop at the handle end of your grabber.

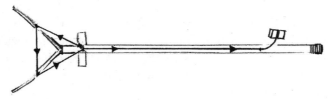

To make the blades snap open, you will need two sturdy rubber bands. Loop one end through the eye hook on the outside of one the blades and pass it through the rubber band again so that it is secure. Loop the other end over the eye hook on the same side of the crosspiece. Repeat for the other blade. Things just seem to slip from varnished blades, so hot glue pieces of foam padding from an old helmet at the ends of the blades to improve the grabbing ability. By this point, you should be in grabbing mode, so go start building your spaceship.

# Sling Chair

**Y**ou have played hard, busted a stick, and ripped your pants. Sounds as if you're ready for a rest in a comfy sling chair. To make one, you'll need an old pair of hockey pants with the pads and protectors, two broken hockey sticks (choose really strong ones with carbon fibre or fibreglass reinforcement because your safety will depend on their strength), a 75' skein of 1/4" nylon rope, an 8' piece of 1/2" nylon cord, at least 12 metal grommets (plastic grommets will pop out), and three 11" cable ties. Tools required are a drill, a 1/4" drill bit, a hammer and a grommet setter. You will also have to do some surgery on the pants, followed up by a bit of sewing. You can talk an experienced stitcher into doing that part for you, or you can do it yourself — just get permission before messing with someone else's sewing machine! This chair will not support anyone who weighs more than 170 pounds, nor will it endure bouncing and hijinks. It is meant for simple, peaceful relaxation.

The success of this project, as with most worthy adventures, lies in the state of the seat of the pants. Carefully inspect the seams to see that they are in good shape. If they are not, find another pair, or reinforce the seams with machine stitching. Take out the thigh protector plates and put them aside for later. If there is lacing in the fly, remove it. Then, using an X-acto knife or seam ripper, open the front of the pants from the bottom of the fly opening to the crotch. Some pants have a padded protector behind the

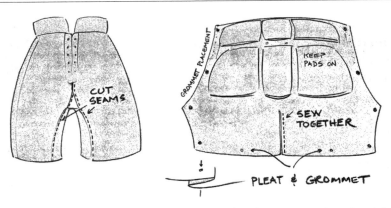

front laces. Cut this off; you don't need it for this project. Cut along the seam to and around the crotch panel, and then down the inside seam of each pant leg. At this point the former pants should now be an open piece of cloth. You can now sew together the open edges of the former leg seams at the centre of the piece. This will require several passes on the sewing machine to make it strong.

Lay the piece down flat so that the interior hip padding is facing you. When the seat is completed, the waist seam will be at the front of the chair. The pants legs seam will run up the back of the seat. At 8" out from both sides of the centre seam, gather a 2" deep pleat and put a grommet through it. At this point the seat should be taking form. Place four grommets evenly spaced along each outside edge of the fabric, folding the fabric over so that you are always going through at least two layers. Once all the grommets are in place, make sure no sharp edges are exposed.

Now you are ready to start assembling your sling chair. Cut a piece of hockey stick 40" long. On the wide side, drill a series of five 1/4" holes, 1 1/2" inches apart, 1" from the ends of the stick. Cut two pieces of 1/4" rope 15' long. Singe the ends so that they will thread through the holes easily and will not fray.

From this point, your work will be much easier if the chair is suspended freely and not against a wall. I used a chin-up bar and that worked just fine. Loop the 8' long 1/2" cord around each end of the stick and suspend it. For the back support, cut a piece of stick 20" long. Drill a hole near each end of the stick. Take one of the 15' pieces of 1/4" nylon rope and tie a sturdy knot at the first grommet, then thread it through the stick, the next grommet and so on, leaving 30" of rope per span. Tie off through the fourth grommet and around the back support piece with a sturdy knot through the hole. Now do the other side. Adjust these ropes until you get satisfactory support and position. Don't get in the chair yet, though. You have some more stringing to do. There should be two remaining holes on either side of the top support stick. Cut two pieces of rope 36" long, and thread one end through the hole and tie a knot. This rope will loop through the back support plates (the plastic thigh guards) and attach to the remaining grommet holding the pleat.

Leave the padding on the thigh guard pieces. Drill one of them in all four corners and the other in only two top corners as it sits horizontally. This can be done easily by drilling through the guard pieces into a piece of scrap wood. Usually these thigh guards have two holes in them towards the centre, so if yours don't, you'll have to drill some. Run a cable tie through the top from the back, through the lower hole and back around the back support stick. With two other cable ties, attach the top corners of the lower panel to the lower corners of the top panel. Thread the loose remaining lines through the corner holes in the top back support and tie through the remaining grommet.

At this point you are almost done — you just need a foot rest. Cut a stick 14" long, and drill holes in each end with the 1/4"

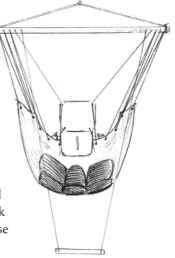

drill bit. Cut two pieces of nylon rope 60" long. Thread the rope through the foot rest and tie a knot so it doesn't slip through. At the other end, go through the remaining holes and knot likewise. To get the right degree of comfort, you will have to do some adjusting once the lines have stretched. Your behind should be a little lower than your knees. Now, grab a book and a drink and enjoy your hard-earned rest. Or you could get right back to work and make three more sling chairs to use around the dinner table.

# Index

# Notes

# Notes

# Notes

*S*truggling to keep their son away from hockey and its detritus, Peter Manchester's parents brought him up in Belgium, Norway, Congo, France, and distant parts of the United States. But they couldn't stop his tinkering; with alarming frequency, he transformed household items into unrecognizable jumbles, upon which he practiced his improvisational skills. At last, in 1992, overcome by the pull of hockey, Manchester moved to Sackville, New Brunswick.

When he takes a break from reincarnating derelict hockey gear, Peter Manchester is a well-known painter and illustrator. This Leonardo of Laminated Sticks first stretched the bounds of glue, duct tape, and good taste in his best-selling book *50 Things to Make with a Broken Hockey Stick*. Thanks to that success, the supply of broken sticks around his local arenas dwindled. Undaunted, he turned to other resources, and *Fabulous Fabrications from Busted Hockey Gear* is the result.

Visit Peter Manchester's website at www.petermanchester.ca.